HOW TO AVOID THE TEN BIGGEST

HOME-BUYING TRAPS

HOW
TO AVOID
THE TEN
BIGGEST
HOME-BUYING
TRAPS

by A. M. Watkins

New and Revised Edition

Hawthorn Books, Inc.
PUBLISHERS / *New York*

HOW TO AVOID THE TEN BIGGEST HOME-BUYING TRAPS

Design by Ellen E. Gal

NEW AND REVISED EDITION

1   2   3   4   5   6   7   8   9   10

Foreword to the New and Revised Edition

A few years ago the United States Senate subcommittee on housing held special hearings in Washington, D.C., on the subject of defective housing and what could be done to protect home-buyers from bad houses. The author of this book, among others, was asked to testify. To any experienced observer of the housing industry it seemed as if history were repeating itself, for most of the problems aired at the hearings—poor heating, wet basements, shoddy design, and so on—were the very same problems that had caused trouble for home-buyers in the past and have continued to cause trouble in the years since. Such problems form a pattern, and the realization of this fact prompted this book.

Here, therefore, are the most common mistakes, or traps, continually made in houses along with how to avoid them when you shop for a house, whether the house is new or old. This is not to say that most houses are deficient or defective. No one has ever truly documented the incidence of flawed or unflawed houses in the United States. In all probability many new houses are reasonably well built, though not necessarily perfect or even near perfect. On the whole, used houses may be a little more subject to structural drawbacks if only because of natural wear and tear over the years. There are also used houses that are excellent values.

By knowing a few basic facts about house design and construction, however, any interested home-buyer can be alerted to the most common defects likely in houses and how to detect them when shopping for a house. The purpose of this book is to lay out before you how to do this, how to judge the quality of a house, and how in the end to buy a reasonably good house at a good price.

This book was originally written and published in 1968. Since then the price of housing in the United States has climbed sharply, chiefly as a result of national inflation induced by the Vietnam war. But also as we entered the 1970's, important innovations were being made in housing, and new kinds of housing were being introduced. Low-cost mobile homes were being mass-produced and sold chiefly as permanent housing by the hundreds of thousands. Industrialization was also taking hold in traditional housing, with growing numbers of houses of conventional design and construction being turned out inside house factories.

More and more new types of houses, such as the so-called town houses, were being built in nearly every part of the country. The modern town house is an up-to-date version of the old familiar row house. It had its origin in colonial days as truly a town house in the downtown sections of such cities as Boston, New York, Philadelphia, and Baltimore.

Innovations were also being made in land planning and the overall design of housing developments, and whole new towns of housing were being built from scratch. There is "cluster housing" and the Planned Unit Development, or PUD (consisting of a mix of different kinds of houses and housing, often with new built-in village centers and stores). Two notable examples of new towns recently launched in the United States are Columbia, Maryland, and Reston, Virginia. The first was planned for an ultimate population of over 100,000 inhabitants, the second for 75,000.

Regardless of the kind of house you may buy and where it is located, the same basic principles of good design and construction almost always apply. A house is a house whether it is covered with a thatched roof on a Pacific island, or whether it is a Cape Cod bungalow built three hundred years ago or new today. As a matter of fact, one of those seemingly fragile thatched-roof houses in the Pacific can be quite durable for its climate and often embodies the very same design principles to thwart its climate and the same structural defenses to thwart ground termites as those employed for the same purposes in a modern well-built American house; these are among the important things to know about buying a house which are described in this book, specifically in these instances in Chapters 5, 8, and 9.

Here, then, is not necessarily all you should know before you buy a house but instead some vital things to know in order to avoid the most common pitfalls and traps that can be lying in wait for the unsuspecting home-buyer. In addition, here also are things to know about highly desirable features to seek in a house.

A good house can offer you far more than mere shelter from the rain, wind, and cold, though many houses unfortunately offer little more. A really good house can be a joy and a pleasure to live in and can provide a continual source of delight. The purpose of this book is to tell you how to step from that first category, the ordinary house, to that second category, the superior house, and as a result, attain a high level of living satisfaction and pleasure, day in and day out, from the house you buy.

A.M.W.

Contents

HOW TO AVOID THE TEN BIGGEST
HOME-BUYING TRAPS

This modest house is of great value (and price) because of its commanding location overlooking the Atlantic Ocean. (*Techbuilt*)

The High-Priced House

We are going to plunge right in with a story. It illustrates how to buy a house at a fair price. Though it concerns the purchase of a used house, it can also help you if you are in the market for a new house. This book will deal evenly with the buying of both new and old houses, though old houses (all ages) account for roughly seven out of every ten houses bought and sold each year.

The story has to do with Jack Briggs and his wife, who had been shopping for a house for three months when they found the one they wanted. It was an older house owned by a man named Wilson. It was for sale at $38,500. Jack doubted that it was worth that much, so he hired a real-estate appraiser to appraise it. The man figured that the house was worth $35,850, its current market value, he said, and charged Jack a fee of $60.

Jack was a thorough guy; he had learned from past experience. He therefore called in a professional engineer who inspected

1

houses to check the structural condition of the house. This cost
$75, but it was worth it in terms of insurance, if nothing
else. The engineer's report cited a few flaws but nothing overly serious. A new furnace might be needed in a few years, and the house
was not insulated. Some rewiring would be needed, and the foundation needed a little shoring up in one place. The house would
also need a paint job, and Jack's wife figured on a certain amount
of kitchen modernization, though not a whole new kitchen. In
all, Jack calculated that about $3,000 would be required for
repairs and improvements, though he could move in right away.

The house was overpriced, but how much could he get it for?
Armed with known facts about the house, Jack and his wife decided they would pay $35,500 or $36,000, their absolute limit.
Jack told his wife he would tell Wilson he would give him $33,500
for the house, his first bid.

His wife practically screamed with alarm. She said Mr. Wilson
would be insulted. "He won't speak to us anymore!"

"Hold on," Jack said. "He'll probably turn it down, but we've
got to start low to leave room for negotiations." She continued
to object, and Jack finally said reluctantly that he'd make it
$34,000 but not a penny more on the first go-around.

Jack called Wilson and said he liked the house a lot. Exaggerat-
ing a little, he said it needed about $3,000 to $4,000 worth of
improvements—painting, insulation, and so on. Therefore Jack
simply could not pay $38,500, the asking price. Jack took a
deep breath and told Wilson he would give him $34,000 for the
house.

Wilson laughed. "I'm sorry," he said. "You'll have to do better
than that."

Jack told him, "Think it over, and let me know. If you want
to come down, give me a call." They left it at that.

Jack waited a few days, and sure enough Wilson called back.
He told Jack, "Look, I'd like to sell the house fast. If you want
to do business now, you can have it for thirty-seven thousand, five
hundred—a thousand dollars off the price. Another family is interested, and a broker is bringing them over this afternoon. I like you
and your wife, so I thought I'd call you back and let you know.
Thirty-seven five, that's the best I can do."

Jack said he'd talk it over with his wife and call back.

Jack's wife began to panic. "We'll never get the house now," she said. "Especially if somebody else is seeing it."

"Don't worry," Jack said. "There's always another buyer in the wings. They always say that."

But Jack was concerned, too. Suppose there was another buyer who offered more?

Jack told his wife, "I'll call him back in the morning. Besides, I've got an idea. Two can play the game. I'll just tell him that we're considering another house." Jack added, "Luckily, we're dealing directly with him. He won't pay a broker's commission if he sells to us. If there's really another guy in the picture with a broker, it's going to cost Wilson six percent."

Jack did some figuring on a piece of paper and said, "If the other guy pays the full price, thirty-eight, the broker gets his cut, and Wilson ends up with thirty-six thousand, one hundred ninety net for the house."

His wife said, "That's still more than our offer. We have to meet that."

"No," Jack said. "Chances are the other guy will offer less, too. So Wilson won't get more than about thirty-six thousand net. Probably less."

Jack called Wilson back the next day and said he and his wife would like another look at the house. Jack really wanted to make his next offer face to face with Wilson, rather than on the phone.

At the house Jack and his wife checked a few things and then sat down with Wilson. He braced himself as he prepared to make another offer. He said finally, "We still like the house, but the best we can offer is thirty-five five." Jack waited a moment and added his kicker: "We've been looking at another house we like a lot, but I thought we'd come over here once more and give our last offer. That's the best we can do." He would like to make it higher, he said, but he simply could not.

Wilson said, "I'm afraid that's not enough. I've already come down a thousand dollars, and I'm just not prepared to sell for less." He proceeded to recount all the special features of the house and the things he had done to improve it. He all but said that Jack's offer was unthinkable. They parted amicably.

Wilson had deliberately feigned unconcern. After Jack and his wife left, however, he began wondering if he would ever sell the house. The couple the broker had brought over turned out to be duds. The man had offered a mere $34,000 flat. Of all the nerve, Wilson thought. And the broker would get 6 percent from that. Well, maybe he could come down to $37,000, and Briggs would buy. Who knows?

If not, however, he might not sell the house for months. The market might get tighter, and there weren't many buyers at the moment. Was Briggs kidding about buying another house? He would wait a few days, and maybe Briggs would call. Or else maybe he should phone and come down another five hundred, maybe even a thousand.

He decided to stall a bit (a standard technique). But he did not want to stretch his anxiety too far. If he held firm too long, he might see his only really good prospect take off and buy another house.

Jack and his wife were also nervous, but, Jack reminded himself, that was par for the course during such negotiations. You need a stout heart and a firm hold on your nerves.

Fortunately, Jack and his wife were not compelled to leave their present house. They could take their time. Jack thought that if he held off a few days longer, he might save another five hundred or thousand dollars. He would pay up to $36,000 for the house, but no more unless perhaps Wilson really would not come down.

Things stood that way for several days. Both men fought off the temptation to call the other. Wilson called the broker to see if any other prospective buyer had shown up. The broker said No but that if Wilson came down in price, he might be able to stir up new interest. As of now, he had exhausted every prospect for the house.

Wilson called Jack the next day. He could not hold back any longer. He said, "My wife wants to sell right away, and maybe we still can get together. If you really want the house, you can have it for thirty-six five. How's that?"

Jack avoided a direct answer. They talked for a while, each feeling out the other. Jack's wife, standing at his elbow, urged him to accept Wilson's offer. "I just don't know what to do," Jack said.

A pause. Then Jack said, "Make it thirty-six even, and it's a deal."

Another pause. Wilson said, "Okay, you've got yourself a house. I'll take it."

Jack confirmed his bid in writing and bought the house for that price, an even $36,000, or $2,500 below the original asking price.

Nearly all used houses are subject to bargaining, and so are some new houses, as you'll see in a moment. A further fact is that you can save more money on a house by knowing how to bargain and knowing how to avoid the high-priced house than you can in any other way. Any skeptic still unconvinced of this or of the extent of overpriced houses should consider the following true cases.

A couple we know wanted to buy a house priced at $30,000. It had a superb river view, though the house itself was small and no great shakes. They could not afford $30,000 and were ready to give up on it when just for a lark they offered $25,000. Their offer was snapped up. It made them think that they should have offered even less!

Another house, a fine old English Tudor showplace, was put on the market for $68,500. The owner claimed he had put that much money into it, and the house was in good condition. Months went by with no takers. One man was on the verge of offering $50,000, but he backed away at the last minute. Even that was more than he could afford. He heard later that the house was sold shortly afterward for, of all things, $39,000!

This example also points up the high importance of the location of a house. The house was located in a distant suburb of a large city, formerly an area of rolling countryside. In the decades following World War II, however, the large showplace was overtaken by urban sprawl, surrounded more and more by development houses in the $35,000 to $40,000 price range. Nobody with $60,000 to $70,000 to spend for a house wanted to live there. The value of the old house was undercut by the new houses being built nearby for less than half its former value.

A transferred business executive was interested in buying a $56,500 house, according to *The Wall Street Journal* in one of its periodic reviews of the housing market. The house was not that desirable, so the man made a token offer of $45,000. The broker called him back and said, "Congratulations, you've bought yourself a house!"

Why High-Priced Houses?

There are three main reasons for high-priced houses. First, many an owner has a wildly inflated idea about the value of his house. He sets the price at a very high level in relation to realistic value, and then he sometimes adds a little more just for extra profit. Sometimes such people will get their price from an unsuspecting buyer, their fond hope. In many such cases, however, the house goes unsold for months if not years. Ultimately the owner sells for less and often considerably less.

Second, the house is not worth the price asked because its location has lost value. The neighborhood deteriorates, or lower-priced houses are built nearby. The house itself may be worth a high price—too bad it could not be moved bodily to an area more befitting its type of house—but nobody wants it at its present location unless it is marked down.

Third, many owners, more realistically inclined, anticipate a heady set of negotiations. They deliberately set their price up a little high to give themselves a cushion to work with when a serious buyer comes along. Perhaps someone with money to throw away will pay the high price with no dickering. That's great. They'll be delighted to accept the money. But more often such owners come down in price and are perfectly reasonable about it. They sell for what they originally wanted, or fairly close to the basic value of their houses.

How Do You Avoid an Overpriced House?

The first thing to do in avoiding an overpriced house is to determine how much a house is really worth. Knowing this is vital, whether you're buying a new house or an old one. If you're not

Above: This handsome California house will surely increase in value over the years because of its excellent design in addition to its highly desirable location in the Pasadena Hills. *Below:* Floor plan shows excellent room arrangement and zoning. The designer is architect Neill Nobel. (*George de Gennaro; illustrations courtesy* Better Homes & Gardens, © *Meredith Corporation, 1966*)

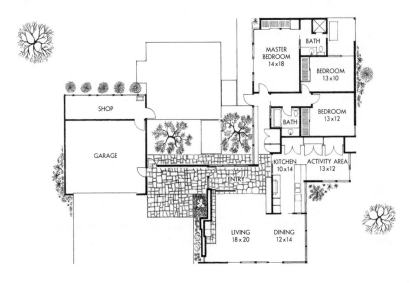

8 TRAP NUMBER 1

inclined to bargain, determine what a house is worth, offer that much, and that's all. The seller can accept it or not.

To find out is easy: Simply hire a real-estate appraiser to appraise the house for you, as Jack Briggs did. The fee will generally range from $50 to $75, more or less, depending on house price and the standard fees in your area.

Appraisers are listed in the yellow pages of the telephone book under "Real Estate Appraisers" or "Appraisers—Real Estate." You can also call a local bank or the real-estate board for recommendations. The best appraisers are usually members of the Society of Real Estate Appraisers or of the American Institute of Real Estate Appraisers. When you call an appraiser, ask if he is a member of either. If not, try for one who is.

An appraiser computes the "fair market value" of a house according to three main factors: (1) the cost of rebuilding the same house at current building rates, less depreciation; (2) the value of the house site—its lot—which depends greatly on prevailing land values in the area; and (3) the prices comparable houses have recently been selling for in the area. He adds the first two figures together (house plus lot) and adjusts in accordance with the third factor to come up with a total value for the particular house.

You can also learn about current house values by keeping your eyes open and asking questions when you shop for a house. Some people study the market, read the real-estate ads and compare prices, check new house prices, and find out what used houses have sold for recently. They end up with an acquired sense of values for houses. On seeing a house they instinctively have a good idea of what it's worth.

If you're buying a used house, you may wonder what the owner paid for it. He won't always tell you, of course, but you can still find out. You go to the real-estate deed files at City Hall or the county courthouse. Tell the clerk you wish to see the deed filed on the house. Anyone can see it. The previous sales price may not be given, but it can generally be determined from the tax stamps on the deed. The federal tax, for example, may run $1.10 per $1,000. Thus $22 worth of stamps on the deed shows that the house was sold last for $20,000 ($22 divided by $1.10, times 1,000).

A fine old house like this eighteenth-century colonial house can be worth virtually any price (in satisfaction as well as in money). Note the excellent proportion and symmetry of its design. It is the Julius Deming House, Litchfield, Connecticut, built in 1790, a classic example of Federal architecture. (*Wayne Andrews*)

The Importance of Location

Because location exerts a powerful influence on the value of houses, it rates a few more words. Many of us have seen houses that command premium prices because they're on a lovely lake frontage or in a highly desirable "name" area. There's Grosse Pointe outside of Detroit, Shaker Heights outside of Cleveland, River Oaks in Houston. A virtually identical house a few miles away in a so-so location will sell for considerably less. The location makes the difference.

The reverse situation is the house that may be an excellent buy except—and here's when to beware—it is located in a neighborhood that is quietly going downhill. You may not know it, but the old-timers are fleeing; commercial development is slated to begin soon. All the old houses are eroding away in value simply because of a developing change for the worse. There may be few visible signs of the downhill slide to the inexperienced eye, but it could be going on nevertheless. This puts special emphasis on checking the value of a house in an area that's unfamiliar to you.

On the other hand, some houses can represent quite a bargain buy in an area or neighborhood that in the opposite way was formerly considered undesirable but is slowly and inexorably on the upgrade. It may be an area benefiting from renewal or simply one that has been out of fashion but is coming back by its bootstraps. Some classic examples are found in old sections of large cities that have been coming back in recent years, such as the West (Greenwich) Village in New York, where many houses have increased sharply in value in recent years. Latch on to a good house in such a place before the neighborhood improvement becomes generally known, and often you can get yourself quite a buy.

It's also important to check on the local zoning rules, assuming you don't want to see those lovely woods across the street invaded by bulldozers someday to make way for a new shopping center or chemical factory. Your best protection is an area that is strictly zoned chiefly for residential use, permitting little or no other kind of development. If there are commercial and industrial zones nearby, watch out.

You should, in fact, be particularly wary of buying a house near any sizable piece of vacant, undeveloped land. Unless there are firm plans for the development of that land, who knows what will happen to it? If it is later developed for commercial use or for cheap housing, it could sharply downgrade the value of the rest of the area around, including your house.

Among other things, check on how zealously the local politicians guard the zoning regulations. If they have a past record of allowing little or no down-zoning of residential property (to allow the cheapest house or other construction), that's fine. But if they're fast and loose with the zoning rules, they're likely to be fast and loose with what they allow to be built near the house you buy.

Buying Strategy

Now let's assume you have found a house you'd like to buy. You've checked on the value, the neighborhood, and other such things (as detailed in later chapters). You're almost ready to make a bid. Before you do, try to determine how long the house has been on the market, a telling fact. The longer it has gone unsold, the more likely the owner will take a reduced price, and the lower your first offer can be.

To get a house at the lowest possible price, however, you must be prepared to lose it to a possible higher bidder. In any case, start low, and don't worry too much. You can always come back with a higher bid—and come back a third time even higher. If you're averse to bargaining, have a broker or your lawyer do it for you. Or you can decide on the price you are willing to pay,

Spacious old Carpenter Gothic house built in 1894 has five bedrooms and splendid view overlooking the Hudson River. (*All About Houses*)

and offer that. There are also certain people, astutely business-minded in other ways, who simply cannot face up to personal confrontation concerning money. They tend to pay whatever is asked for a house (or anything else being bought) largely because of emotional makeup.

Though verbal bids play a big part in the various stages of negotiating for a house, they are not necessarily binding. In many cases a bid must be in writing to be legally binding. The wording of the bid is also critical, and it's a good idea to have this checked by a lawyer. You don't have to make a big production of the bid, however. Just be sure it conforms with your intentions and that you are protected and can pull out of the deal if, for example, the house turns out to have serious structural defects or if, say, you subsequently cannot obtain a satisfactory mortgage.

For houses priced up to about $25,000 to $35,000 the first bid can be at least 10 to 20 percent under the asking price. The higher the asking price, the more you can underbid. For houses priced over $35,000 or so, there are no general rules to go by. Things are wide open, with some being bought for as much as 50 percent under the asking price, as the cases noted earlier testify.

The price a house will sell for depends much on current market conditions, including the availability of mortgage money. If mortgages are easy to obtain, people can often buy a house they otherwise could not buy. The state of the stock market is also a factor. When the market is going well, it exerts a favorable psychological influence and an indication of both general prosperity and a greater supply of people with money, and conversely.

It also depends on such things as whether or not an owner is in a hurry to sell. In sum, it comes down to supply and demand, as with other products for sale. Such facts are good to remember when you shop for a house. They can give you a sixth sense for houses.

Other Facts to Remember

The asking price for a house is either the highest price the owner hopes to get or simply his starting point for negotiations, or both. A classified ad for the house may state "Asking Price . . ."

and give a figure. Usually the owner will be receptive to any reasonable offer. He also may say, "Make an offer."

Some sellers say their price is "firm." They imply they will settle for no less—or so they hope, often wishfully. If they don't get their price, however, many will face reality and come down. Others may take their houses off the market, and still others will indeed get huffy should someone make what they consider a ridiculously low offer. They feel their houses are worth every single dollar they ask. Such a house may or may not be worth the price, but it is up to you to decide. If it is worth the price, you must pay it or something close to it. More often than not, however, such people have delusions of grandeur. Their houses are sorely overpriced.

The New House

A custom-house builder we know put a large new house up for sale at $42,500. The house did not sell for a while; the market was sluggish. He advertised more, but still no sale. A man came along and offered $37,500. The builder said No, but he would take $38,500, and the house was sold. The builder took what he could get rather than keep the house any longer.

That's the kind of new house, the already finished, speculatively built kind, that is most likely to be overpriced. It's therefore the new house that is most likely to be subject to bargaining, particularly if it has gone unsold for a while. It costs builders money every month to keep the houses, so as time goes by they are increasingly open to any reasonable offer. Naturally, a builder is much tempted to overprice a new house with the hope of getting as much as possible at first. If it doesn't sell, he will ordinarily have to come down in price, taking the best price he can get.

That's why a low first bid can save you money when you buy a speculative-builder house. You may be turned down, but you can come back with a higher offer. On the other hand, you may be amazed at how much you might save on the house.

New houses in a new development are much more likely to be firm in price. Generally you must pay the listed price, particularly for a new house that you order from the builder's model which he will build for you in the development. An exception is when a builder is closing out a tract of houses and has a few remaining houses, already finished, that he wants to unload. This is especially true if the houses have been standing unsold for a long time.

Real-Estate Brokers

A veteran home-buyer we know now holds a dim view of brokers. He and his wife were being driven to a house by a broker who lauded to the skies its every characteristic. "It's an unbeatable buy," the broker said, reeling off one glowing feature after another. To our friend the house sounded increasingly familiar. He finally said, "It sounds like the Evans house. Another broker showed it to us."

The broker instantly turned the car around and without breaking verbal stride, proceeded to reel off all the things that were wrong with the house. He heard that it had termites and, among other things, that the furnace was in bad shape. The Evans house was definitely not for them, but he could take them to another, far better house!

Our friend decided to profit from the experience. To learn about possible flaws in a house for sale, he would casually mention the house to brokers other than the one who had shown him the house, stating frankly that he was interested in the house but had seen it through another broker. He says, "It's amazing how much you can learn about a house from a broker who can't sell it to you."

Of course, not all brokers are as shameless. In fact, brokers can help you in many positive ways. A good broker can help you negotiate and bargain for a house, a boon if you are averse to bargaining. He can help you find a house that is otherwise unobtainable, because some owners list their houses exclusively with brokers.

You can use one or more brokers and also shop on your own. A home-buyer is not tied exclusively to one. The broker's fee is paid by the seller (out of the sales price paid for the house). The usual fee is 6 percent of the sales price, 10 to 12 percent for farms and rural properties. You should know the fee in your area. Ask any broker.

Though most brokers deal chiefly with used houses, some handle new houses for builders. Many houses may be listed with brokers, but the owners also have the right to sell directly to a buyer. If you learn about a house for sale without a broker, ordinarily you can buy it at its net price—that is, the asking price less what the seller would have paid the broker. Remember this, because many sellers raise their prices to allow for the broker's commission.

Some houses are listed exclusively with a broker for ninety days, sometimes longer. If the broker has an exclusive, he may still be entitled to his commission even if you buy the house without going through him. It depends on the owner's agreement with the broker. If you are directed to a house by a broker, you must buy it through him. Some cagey owners will try to evade the broker's fee by suggesting you deal with them secretly to eliminate the broker's fee. This is not only dishonest but illegal. If you buy the house, the broker is entitled to be paid, and you might be held liable. And if a broker takes you to a house you have seen before, don't enter it. Simply say you've already seen it.

Choosing a Broker

There are brokers, and there are brokers. In all, there are about 500,000 licensed real-estate brokers in the country. Many are part-time hacks, including cabdrivers, both good and not so good, part-time housewife brokers, part-time carpenters, service-station owners, and the like. By and large, the best are the 100,000 or so realtor members of the National Association of Real Estate Boards. A broker can call himself a realtor only if he is a member and hence a member also of the local real-estate board. Though many nonrealtor brokers may be top-notch, in general the full-time realtors carry the most listings and tend to know the most about the local market.

In addition to helping you find a house and negotiating the sale for you, a good broker can also help you find a mortgage and tell you about such things as the closing costs. Never forget, though, that he is hired by the seller. Naturally, he strives to obtain the best price for his client (the seller). One of them, therefore, may have you believe that the price is firm, though you wish to offer less and perhaps considerably less. Despite the cries of pain from the broker, tell him the price you want to bid, however low, and he is duty bound to deliver it to the owner.

On the other hand, he wants to make the sale, for otherwise he earns no fee. A good broker will therefore strive for a meeting of minds, a price acceptable to both buyer and seller. Sometimes a buyer and seller will reach an impasse, with neither willing to budge over the price gap between them. At this stage brokers will work hard for a compromise, including an occasional low-voiced offer to share their commission in order to achieve a compromise. Though realtors are honor bound not to cut their commissions, they have been known to do it.

You should also remember that very few brokers are construction experts, so whatever one says, usually with great enthusiasm, about the outstanding structural condition of a house, it should be discounted heavily. "Look at all the insulation you'll get from those big thick stone walls," one may say, obviously totally ignorant of the fact that solid masonry has very little insulating value. Go to a construction expert for such opinions, not to a broker. A real-estate broker is expected to know no more about construction than a Wall Street broker is expected to know about computer circuits when he sells you stock in IBM.

On the other hand, many brokers are honorable and will even point out possible flaws in houses. Well established in their business, they would prefer that you know about the house before you buy, rather than let a bad sale boomerang. Besides, they also make hay psychologically by telling you some of the bad as well as the good. The fact that a broker will come clean and reveal flaws to you can be impressive evidence that he is dealing fairly and squarely. This can earn him your confidence, and he knows it. Besides, nearly every house has flaws, and we all know it.

Before Buying a House

Let's say you've decided to buy a house. You've investigated it, the price is right, and you're ready to buy. To seal the deal, a signed binder on the house with token deposit, say, $50 to $100 is usually required. Tread carefully here, for that binder may mean

Overpriced house? It depends on its location as well as its structural condition. This house might sell for $20,000 in one area and over $25,000 in another. (*Maynard L. Parker*)

nothing at all. If the seller gets a better offer the next day, you can be left in the cold.

On the other hand, you may change your mind, but even if you signed a mere scrap of paper and put down a piddling deposit, you may be as legally bound to buy the house as if you had signed a thirty-page document. It depends on the wording of the agreement signed. That's why it's best to enlist the aid of a good real-estate lawyer before signing anything.

The next step is usually a conditional sales contract drawn up between buyer and seller. You agree to buy the house at a certain price by a certain date, conditional on obtaining a satisfactory mortgage. Another condition to insist on is that the house be in sound structural condition, as determined by a construction expert hired by you. Still another is to include the outside date at which a new house is to be completed and ready for occupancy for you. With an existing house it is the outside date at which the seller is to be out so you can move in; if he's not out, the rent he will pay you should be stipulated. The signing of a conditional sales contract also requires, generally, a cash down payment, the amount of which may vary. If the deal falls through for good reason, the contract should also state that the money is to be returned in full to the buyer. If the buyer reneges without a valid reason, however, he can lose his payment.

The amount of the down payment, or deposit, at this stage is customarily 5 to 10 percent of the sales price, though sometimes $50 or $100 is enough. Actually, it is the most money the buyer is willing to give and the least the seller is willing to take. And it's mainly a clear-cut indication of your willingness to buy, since you are putting your money on the line. Later when you arrange for a mortgage, however, and close the deal for the house, the mortgage lender will require a stipulated minimum down payment. The sum depends on the type and amount of mortgage you get, and as described in Chapter 3, it can range anywhere from nothing up to 30 or 40 percent down.

Other important considerations can weigh heavily on the deal, depending on the house and on such things as the real-estate customs and laws in your area. Remember, though, you want a house and not a lawsuit, which puts additional importance on consulting a good real-estate lawyer when you prepare to buy a house.

The price of housing will fluctuate from time to time according to supply and demand, though in recent years it seems as if house prices could go upward only. House prices in many areas increased by 3 to 5 percent a year during the last decade. This sharp inflation was due almost entirely to American involvement in Vietnam which, as everybody knows, also unleashed strong inflationary price rises in other areas of American life. As a result, many houses that were worth $25,000 to $30,000 ten years ago have recently been valued at $35,000 to $45,000, and prices are still going up at this writing. Realistically speaking, one must face up to the price spiral in houses, though at the same time one can and should beware of the overpriced house.

Not all houses, however, were going up in price. In some areas, such as Seattle, Washington, there were pockets of economic depression which affected housing as well as other local prices. By the early 1970's many houses were available there at prices notably less than the prices for comparable houses in many other areas of the country. (Seattle's biggest industry, the Boeing Corporation, had mass layoffs which cast an economic pall over that area.) If you are moving to a part of the country unfamiliar to you, finding out about the local housing market before you buy a house can be important. The local housing market, in fact, can be quite different from that of other areas as little as one hundred miles away.

Although construction costs had been rising steadily in recent years, home-builders were fighting back at inflation with new techniques and new kinds of houses that reduced costs. One example is the town house, a modern version of the old row house, which can be built for less money than a traditional one-family house because it (the town house) requires less expensive land per house and also because its construction cost can be reduced as a result, among other things, of the party walls between adjacent houses.

How do you get a good house at a fair price? The price depends, of course, on the size and type of house and its location. But if you know how to evaluate the basic worth of any house and, if necessary, an expert's appraisal of the worth of a particular house is obtained, you can go a long way toward getting a good house at a fair price. You also want to avoid paying an excessive price—or any price—for a low-quality house. How to do this and how to judge design and structural quality of a house are described in detail in following chapters.

The Unforeseen Expenses
of Buying and Owning a House

A few years ago a group of families in a midwestern development read in the local paper that their school taxes were going up by over $150 a year per house. A multimillion-dollar bond for a new school had been approved, and naturally the bond had to be paid off. Not long afterward, the same homeowners were each hit with a special assessment, averaging some $79 per house, for a new sewer plant. Within three years these and other tax hikes had raised their annual home-ownership costs by close to $500 a year.

Their experience is by no means unique. Home-buyers throughout the country have found to their distress that there can be quite a lot of "unforeseen" expenses when you buy a house, particularly when you buy a house in a growing new community. After all, somebody has to pay for all the new services—waterlines, sewers, and new streets, to name a few—as well as the schools required for children of new residents.

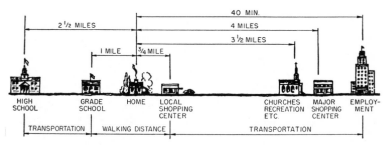

Maximum distances recommended for the location of a house in relation to the essential needs of a typical family (*U.S. Savings & Loan Association*)

Such expenses can mount up high, but they need not. How large or small these expenses are depends on the house you buy, where it is located, and what you do in advance to forestall or minimize those that can be controlled.

Consider Closing Costs First

You will pay closing costs when you buy the house. They are the inevitable costs covering the transaction of buying and are paid on the day you close the deal for a house. They go for various items, small and large, and may total only $100 to $200 if you're lucky. But they may be as much as $500 to $1,000, sometimes more, and usually they must be paid with cash in hand, in addition to the money paid to buy the house.

Closing costs, sometimes called settlement costs, are the admission fee you pay at the door before being allowed in to buy a house. They've come under growing assaults from critics in past years, and eventually a ceiling will probably be put on them. Magazines like *The American Home, Better Homes & Gardens, The Reader's Digest,* and *Redbook,* among others, have attacked them for being arbitrary and excessive, and in early 1972 the Washington *Post* ran a series of articles exposing them. The *Post* reported, for example, details of kickbacks to lawyers which jacked up closing costs paid by home-buyers. Those articles stung, since they were in a paper that was widely read by congressmen. They prompted cries for a congressional investigation of the whole matter of closing costs, even though the Department of Housing and Urban Development (HUD) had a few years before completed a broad study of closing costs that showed much the same pattern of high charges. HUD did not do much, however, until after the clamor following the *Post*'s disclosures. In February, 1972, HUD officials announced that a ceiling would be put on the closing costs that could be charged to a family buying a house with government-insured financing, like FHA mortgages. More action can be expected to reduce closing costs.

Here is a breakdown of the actual closing costs paid by the buyer of a $35,000 house. He bought it with a $9,000 down payment and a $26,000 mortgage loan (plus $1,226 in cash for the closing costs). Note how many are related to the mortgage.

Mortgage commitment fee, ½ of 1% of mortgage, covering appraisal fee, credit report, other such items	$ 130
Title search and title insurance	264
Legal fee for mortgage lender's (bank's) lawyer	250
State mortgage tax, ½ of 1% of mortgage in New York (not imposed in all states)	130
Mortgage recording fee	6
Recording of deed	5
Survey of property	125
Reimbursement to seller for real-estate property taxes paid by him in advance	228
Cost of taking over existing fire and hazard insurance on house	88
Total	$1,226

The specific items in the closing costs will vary from house to house and state to state. They may or may not include all the items noted for that one transaction; they could also include others that this man did not pay. Let's analyze each.

Mortgage commitment fee or service charge. Sometimes it's called a mortgage fee or broker's fee. Some mortgage-lenders charge a flat ½ of 1 percent of the mortgage amount. Others a straight fee, perhaps $100 to $200. It can vary all over the ball field, depending on the lender and the customary charge made in an area. It pays for such things as the money spent by the lender to appraise the house, a credit check on the borrower, and various paper-work items required to prepare the mortgage loan. Sometimes each of these items is individually itemized and charged to you separately; then there is no blanket mortgage fee.

Sometimes the mortgage fee is absorbed in part by the builder or the lender. This depends on the availability of mortgages at a given time. If they are in tight supply, the cost of obtaining one goes up. But if mortgage money is plentiful, lenders vie for your business and will often absorb part or all of the fee. When you shop for a mortgage, ask about the mortgage service fee. Merely asking and even hinting that you may go elsewhere for your mortgage may prompt the lender to give you a break. It depends on how much he wants your business.

Title search and insurance. The real-estate records in the county courthouse are checked to be sure that the seller has a clear title to the property being sold. Most mortgage lenders also require a title-insurance policy to protect their interest in the property should questions arise about the title.

There are two kinds of title policies. The first, the *mortgagee* policy, protects the mortgage lender only and is usually mandatory. The second, the *mortgagor,* or *fee,* policy, is optional. It protects you, the buyer. Getting this one, too, is recommended. It can usually be had for about $100, more or less (in addition to the cost of the mortgagee policy), if you ask for it in advance of closing day.

In some areas of the country it's customary for the seller of the house to pay for the title search and insurance. That makes sense, considering that the seller should vouch for the title to the property he is selling. In other areas the title search and insurance fee are subject to bargaining between buyer and seller. The seller, including some builders, can often be induced to absorb part or all of the expense. In still other cases the buyer pays. There may be little you can do about it.

At the very least try to get the seller to pay it. If you are buying an old house, title-insurance costs can sometimes be reduced by obtaining a reissue of the owner's existing title policy on the house.

Some title companies will replace the existing policy with a new policy at a discount price.

Legal fee for the mortgage lender's (bank's) lawyer. This charge often stirs resentment, but a lawyer is often essential. An enormous amount of legal paper work may be required, involving much time and effort. (Don't necessarily curse the lawyer, however. The blame should be placed on state legislators who have perpetrated a hodgepodge of antiquated laws regulating the transfer of real estate.)

The legal fee can range from about $50 to as much as 1 percent of the house price, depending on the intricacies of the transaction. You may also desire your own lawyer to be present on closing day or at least for consultation earlier. That will mean an additional fee, of course.

"Odds and ends" fees. These include the state and federal taxes on the transaction and the cost of recording the mortgage and deed at the local courthouse. They cannot be avoided. A survey plan of the property may be required. With luck the seller may already have one, or you can get him to pay for it. In some areas it is customary to pay the seller for such things as the heating oil in the tank, but you can claim that such items are part of the house being sold, as is, with no charge to you.

Taxes, escrow money, and insurance. You must pay your share of the city, town, county, state, and school taxes. They are usually paid annually and therefore already paid up on a house by the seller through the next annual payment date for each. You therefore reimburse the seller for the proportion of these taxes he has paid in advance. Your share, paid on closing day, is prorated from the date of purchase to the next due date for each tax.

Escrow money is what you prepay for taxes and sometimes for the house insurance, too. The mortgage lender collects it on closing day and disperses it as it becomes due. Sometimes you are required to pay it in advance (closing day), and there is little you can do to avoid it. Other times you need not pay it till it becomes due.

You can save money on insurance, however, if you arrange beforehand for your own homeowners insurance policy. It's called just that—a homeowners policy. It's sold by many insurance companies. Its cost is usually less than the cost of individual fire, theft, and liability policies on a house. It gives you blanket coverage on these three different hazards. Fire insurance is usually the only policy that you are required to provide on a house you buy. You must obtain the other coverages yourself at extra cost. Get them all together in one policy, and you save money (and also get better insurance protection). The conditional sales contract for a house often includes a fine-print clause saying that the buyer will take over the existing fire insurance on the house. Cross this out, and say instead that you'll provide your own insurance.

You can save even more if you have a homeowners policy on your present house and switch it to the new house. If you arrange for your own insurance, however, have it okayed by the mortgage lender in advance of the closing. A few banks, savings and loan associations, and other mortgage lenders, by the way, will have you believe that you must take the insurance they sell. It's part of the mortgage package, they say. Not only is this coercive selling, it is also against the law in many states. You have the right to get your own insurance, although, of course, it should be adequate for the house. It should be equal to the current replacement cost of the house, less the value of the lot, or at the very least, equal to 80 percent of the house replacement cost.

To sum up, brace yourself for closing costs in advance. Get a complete list of what they'll be when you arrange for the house and the mortgage. If they are too steep, assert your bargaining position, and try to get them cut. It can also help to give yourself an out on closing costs before you sign the conditional sales contract for a house. Insert a clause in these papers saying something like: "Total closing costs for the house to be paid by the buyer are not to exceed $——————— [fill in your limit], or the buyer reserves the right to cancel the purchase." Check the wording with your lawyer.

Unforeseen Tax Hikes

The property taxes on a house may run from a few hundred to well over a thousand dollars a year, depending on the assessed valuation of the house and the local tax rate. That's how you pay for local services, including fire and police protection as well as schools, water, and sewers. It's up to you to determine what they are before you buy. Don't, however, necessarily rely on the casual word of a house salesman or a real-estate broker. Find out from the local tax assessor's office. Should you buy a used house, ask to see the owner's most recent tax bills. There are usually separate bills for school taxes, village and/or town taxes, and county and state property taxes.

An increase in taxes is least likely if you buy a house in an established area where few or no new services and new schools will be needed. They are most likely when you move into a growing new area or a new development or both. If new schools, new roads, new sewers, and other such facilities will be needed, taxes are sure to go up, and you must pay your share. It's as simple as that. The greater the local growth expected, the greater the future tax bill to be expected.

An across-the-board hike in the local real-estate tax rate is generally the way you pay for expanded services, such as more police and fire protection and new schools. In addition, there are "special assessments" levied on property-owners to pay for capital improvements, such as new water mains, sidewalks and curbs, new street paving, a garbage plant, even streetlights and fire hydrants, and, usually most expensive of all, a new sewer system for a community. Not all of these can be foreseen, but also remember that they are generally the result of vocal public demand, rather than arbitrary decisions by government officials.

Being hit with a series of such bills can make things financially tough for you, especially if they come on top of home-ownership bills that are already as high as your income will allow. Realistically speaking, therefore, it is a good idea to allow a cushion in your budget to pay for possible tax hikes if you buy a house in a new development or in a rapidly growing area. A visit to the local tax assessor's office can shed light on the prospects for new taxes. How much are the local real-estate taxes expected to rise in the future? What about the likelihood of special assessments in the area? Don't be fooled if someone tells you taxes can't go up because there's a legal ceiling on the tax rate. New services cost money, and the local government can boost taxes by hiking all assessments without changing the tax base.

Just as closing costs have come under sharp attack, fast-climbing property taxes throughout the country have also brought cries of anguish from homeowners. Finally, in the early 1970's court decisions shook up the whole basis on which local property taxes have been levied and collected. Changes are in the works, though as this is written, no one can foresee exactly how the property tax mess will eventually be changed and resolved. Things may even get worse for some people, depending on the community. It appears likely that property taxes, particularly the school tax, will be levied on a statewide basis, rather than on the present system of each local community paying largely for its own schools. This should have a leveling effect, reducing the high taxes paid by people for schools in one area and lifting, at least somewhat, the low school-tax bill paid by others in other areas. In addition, schools in poor areas will probably get more tax money for their schools.

Before you buy a house, therefore, inquire locally about the future prospects for the local property taxes. Are the local property taxes (especially for schools) likely to go up or down and by how much as a result of possible court-mandated changes in how property taxes are levied?

New-House Expenses

A man who bought a $29,500 house in a new development says, "The builder seeded the front lawn but only ten feet in the rear. We got only three bushes in front. A lawn for the rest of the property plus new landscaping cost me $800 after we moved in."

Besides the expenses likely for a lawn and landscaping with a new house, you should also figure on window screens and storm windows (if needed), both of which are not commonly provided by builders. You will also need window shades and curtains, perhaps new appliances, and though not necessarily essential, such things as an attic fan or a privacy fence around the patio. There can be unexpected expenses for new storage cabinets or closet expansion and changes or additions here and there to make the house more suitable. A survey in a New York suburb showed that the buyers of new houses spent an average of $345 for such things in the first year after moving in (versus only $235 spent the first year by the buyers of used houses).

The biggest potential expenses in a new house are those you must pay to correct major design or construction shortcomings. You may find, for example, that the kitchen requires drastic changes or expansion to make it work. Or a new bathroom is essential. Occasionally things go wrong with the house, and the builder cannot or will not repair them. These are clearly the expensive big-ticket items to avoid, and avoiding them calls for a thorough check on the design and construction of the house *before* you buy.

Possible Unforeseen Expenses with a Used House

The most costly unforeseen expenses with a used house are due to old age and obsolescence. In time the water heater or furnace stops running, the structure requires a new roof, or other repairs are necessary. But again, being prepared for them requires a good check on the house before buying (detailed in Chapter 7).

A used house will often need new interior painting and re-decorating; of course, doing these yourself can save money. New window curtains are usually needed (but unlike a new house, window screens and storm windows often come with the house). Find out about this beforehand. On the bright side, a used house usually has a lawn and is landscaped, so these items should not bring on unforeseen expenses.

A Disclaimer

The various expenses that we've just noted should not frighten you. Sometimes they will evaporate down to very little, particularly if you've scouted the house carefully before buying, so don't be scared by imagined bills, and don't necessarily put off buying a house because of them.

It is also good, however, to set aside money you are likely to need to pay for settling into the house you buy, for there is one last big expense trap to avoid: the high interest rates on installment loans that people must take out in order to pay for unforeseen expenses. That brings up the importance of knowing what you can spend for a house.

How Much House Can You Afford?

The usual rule bandied about is that you can afford a house priced up to two and a half times your annual income. A person earning $10,000 a year, therefore, can buy a $25,000 house. Earning $16,000 can get you a $40,000 house, and so on.

But that rule can be way off. Use it at your own peril. It overlooks the fact that property taxes can run a few hundred dollars a year for one house, but two to three times that amount for another house at exactly the same price. It makes no allowance for heating, which can run, say, $30 a month on the average in the North and practically nothing for a similar house in the South. Nor does it make allowance for the fact that mortgage interest rates and carrying charges are considerably higher today than when that moss-backed old rule of thumb was first used.

Some people can spend up to three times their annual income for a house, whereas others should not spend a penny more than twice their income and sometimes even less. The amount you can afford will depend far more on the monthly carrying costs, upkeep, and ownership expenses for a particular house than on the ratio of the house sales price to your income.

Here is a much wiser rule from family financial experts: A family should spend no more than 20 to 25 percent of its monthly income for total housing expenses. Families with incomes of no more than $10,000 a year should stay close to the 20 percent limit; higher-income people can use the higher limit. If you are going up the ladder at your job and have good prospects of making more money in the future, you could stretch the rule and spend a little more. But if you have already reached your peak earnings level or close to it, be prudent and stay within the rule. The 20 to 25 percent rule should cover every item of your home-ownership expenses, including upkeep and maintenance as well as mortgage payments and annual taxes.

Going a step further, total monthly expenses for *basic* housing bills—mortgage payments, property taxes, and insurance—should generally not exceed your gross annual income divided by 60. This is a down-to-earth formula used by many mortgage lenders to determine a family's financial ability to buy a house. A family earning $12,000 gross a year can therefore spend up to $200 a month for basic expenses ($12,000 divided by 60); a family earning $18,000, up to $300 a month, and so on.

The rule says, in effect, that basic housing expenses should not exceed 20 percent of your gross annual income. It allows an additional 5 percent of income for utilities (including heating) and normal upkeep and maintenance.

The rule of 60 is a good yardstick to use when you begin shopping for a house. By giving you a fairly good idea of how much house you can afford, it can help you stay within bounds when you shop for a house. Nonetheless, the rule of 60 is still inexact. Exactly how much you can afford to spend for a house depends on your income less what you must spend each month for all other essential outlays.

Here is how you can figure it. Simply fill in the figures.

1. ADD UP YOUR MONTHLY LIVING EXPENSES
   OTHER THAN FOR HOUSING:

Food	$_____
Clothing	_____
Medical and dental bills	_____
Life and health insurance	_____
Other insurance	_____
Automobile upkeep and insurance	_____
Commuting to work	_____
Entertainment and recreation	_____
Children's school, college expenses	_____
Installment payments, (washer, dryer, other monthly installment payments)	_____
Church and other contributions	_____
Vacation	_____
Hobbies, books, magazines, records	_____
Savings, investments, etc.	_____
Personal gifts, Christmas expenses	_____

Miscellaneous (barber, beauty-shop
    expenses, bathroom supplies)   _____
Any other?   ============
Total living expenses other than for housing $_____

2. DETERMINE MONTHLY INCOME AVAILABLE
   FOR HOUSING:
    Total gross monthly income (omit a working
      wife's income unless she will continue
      to work) $_____
    Deductions for income taxes, Social
      Security, etc.   ============
    Net take-home pay $_____
    Less living expenses   ============
    Total monthly money available for
      housing $_____

3. DETERMINE MONEY AVAILABLE FOR
   MONTHLY MORTGAGE PAYMENTS:
    Total monthly money available for housing
      from line above $_____
    Subtract amount estimated for property
taxes, insurance, and monthly heating,
upkeep, and operating costs. This figure
will vary according to the house and where
you live and must be estimated locally. In
general, you can figure approximately $3
to $6 a month per $1,000 of house price.
But remember that this is an approxima-
tion. Figure $3 for a small town and up to
$6 for a large town or metropolitan suburb.
Later, when you have settled on a house
you may buy, an accurate determination of
the taxes and other monthly ownership
costs for the house should be made and
used here.   ============
    Total money left for monthly mortgage
      payments $_____

How Much Cash Is Needed to Buy a House?

First there's the down payment and closing costs and then cash on the barrelhead for moving and the inevitable settling-in expenses reported in this chapter. In addition to the money needed for the down payment and closing costs, it's usually a good idea to have a cash reserve cushion of at least $500 to $1,000. Many people do it for less; others must spend more. It depends mainly on the unforeseen expenses that may confront you. But on reading this far you should have a good idea of what they may or may not be.

In effect, the actual cost of a new house will run somewhat higher than its sales price. The sales-price figure is what so often misleads people. Add another $1,000 to perhaps $2,000 to it, and you'll get a more accurate estimate of the true cost of a house. That extra money will ordinarily be needed in cash.

The down payment required and what you must spend monthly to repay the mortgage depend on how the house is financed, the subject of the next chapter.

The Tight
Mortgage Bind

The idea of a mortgage scares some people. To others, the money owed on a mortgage represents a huge emotional burden. This should not be.

The American house mortgage represents just about the cheapest consumer loan available today. It is an instrument that has made home ownership attainable for literally millions of families who otherwise could never have bought a house. Moreover, the interest paid on your mortgage, like money paid for your property taxes, is tax-deductible on your income-tax returns.

The money you must pay every month on your house mortgage, however, is usually the biggest single home-buying expense. It may run $116.73 a month for one house, $179.66 for another, or, say, $247.23 a month, to pick some figures at random. Whatever it is, it is fixed at a certain inflexible amount. You must pay it every month until, of course, the mortgage is repaid in full.

Whatever the sum, it may not seem so burdensome at first. The

33

trouble comes later, when that virtually irrevocable sum of money you owe each month begins to take a seemingly larger and larger bite out of your monthly budget. You can't do much about it without losing the house. That's when you can find yourself in a tight mortgage bind.

Many of us tend to assume larger mortgage payments than we can handle in order to pay off the house quickly. Others accept, not without apprehension, the payments offered to us, not knowing that the very same mortgage can often be repaid at a smaller monthly figure. Sure, that may mean a longer time to pay off the house (though that is not always necessarily so, as we will see in a moment). Still others are caught in a tightening mortgage bind as a result of getting stuck with a bad mortgage.

One such pitfall was pointed up not long ago by a group of southern California homeowners who made national headlines when they picketed the local offices of the big insurance company that owned the mortgages on their houses. The company had informed them by letter that the interest rate on their mortgages was being increased ½ of 1 percent. As a result, the monthly payments due each month on their homes would henceforth be increased accordingly.

Naturally the homeowners were up in arms. If anything is supposed to stay fixed, it's the interest on your mortgage, or so you would think. Not so with some mortgages. Some will have a fine-print clause giving the lender the right to increase the interest rate, in which case, of course, your payments are hiked. The insurance company invoked the clause. Insurance companies are major lenders in the mortgage field, but other kinds of lenders may also have the same clause. The clause goes by several names: "variable rate," "adjustable rate," "interest equalization," or "escalator rate" clause. Whatever it is called, the result is the same. The mortgage-holder is free to raise your interest rate. In recent years a number of mortgage-lenders in various states, particularly California, have used the clause to hike interest rates on existing mortgages as much as 15 percent. This brings up two vital points. First, beware of such a clause. Read your contract before you sign it. A possible exception has to do with what is called the variable-interest mortgage. It's a kind of mortgage proposed for evening out the peaks and valleys in mortgage interest rates from year to year. The interest charged on most mortgages is determined at any one time by national money rates and what banks must pay for the money they borrow and the interest rates they pay to depositors. As a result, home mortgage interest rates have fluctuated from as little as 4 percent in the 1950's to as high as 10 percent in the late 1960's and early 1970's.

Interest rates are determined by federal money policies made in Washington combined with the state of the economy, and many economic factors come into play. The result is that at one time home-buyers may obtain mortgages at a comparatively low interest rate; at other times at a comparatively high rate (and then be stuck with such a rate even though mortgage interest rates come down later). To introduce a degree of flexibility, variable-interest mortgages have been proposed, with the interest rate charged you, the home-buyer, being subject to up-and-down changes according to the varying cost of money. How well such mortgages will succeed is difficult to predict. It may be fine if your particular mortgage rate is lowered after you buy a house, because the national cost of money becomes cheaper; not so fine if the reverse occurs because of national money rates going up.

A second important consideration is that you can shop around for a mortgage. You need not take the first one offered or one that the builder of a new house automatically provides. Try other lenders, and seek out the best loan. A little knowledge about the three main kinds of mortgage will help here. They are the Veterans Administration (VA) mortgage, the Federal Housing Administration (FHA) mortgage, and the conventional mortgage.

The VA Mortgage

The well-known Veterans Administration mortgage loan for veterans, also called a GI mortgage, can be obtained from a regular mortgage lender, such as a bank, an insurance company, or a savings and loan association, as well as from the Veterans Administration itself. The VA insures the lender against loss. You should know about it even if you are not a veteran, since you could take over a VA mortgage if you buy a house from a veteran.

The VA mortgage offers a low down-payment schedule (sometimes nothing down), its interest rate is low, and this in turn means low monthly repayments. It also provides special safeguards in the fine print for home-buyers (to protect veterans from abuses). The house must pass certain minimum construction standards set by the VA, which is additional protection.

The interest rate on a VA loan is usually as low as or lower than on any other kind of mortgage. In recent years it has ranged from 6 to 8½ percent, though at any one time it is usually from ¼ to 1 percent less than other mortgages.

The trouble with VA mortgages is that you cannot always get one. That's because of their low interest rate. When mortgage money is tight, lenders can make more money—because of higher interest rates—on regular mortgages and still find all the takers they want. Generally they will not give VA loans at such a time.

If, however, you are a veteran and live in a small town or rural area, you may qualify for a VA mortgage that is obtained directly from the government. Some ten thousand VA "direct" loans are made each year to enable veterans to buy houses in areas where a mortgage is otherwise unobtainable at reasonable terms. You apply to the nearest VA office. Such mortgages can be had up to $17,500 with no down payment. A more expensive house can be bought with a $17,500 direct GI loan, but you put up the difference in cash. A free booklet describing GI loans can be obtained from any VA office or from the Veterans Administration, Washington, D.C. 20420. If you are a veteran you may also qualify for an FHA loan with special features available only to veterans, even though your VA eligibility may have expired. More on this in a moment.

If you are a veteran and once bought a house with a VA mortgage, you may still be eligible to buy another house with another VA mortgage or even refinance the mortgage on your present house with another VA mortgage. This is generally true for any veteran who bought a house with a VA mortgage before May 7, 1968, which is when the government raised the amount of a mortgage insured by the VA from $7,500 to $12,500. Before then, in other words, the government insured only $7,500 of every VA mortgage it okayed, even though the total mortgage you got was greater than that. Right after World War II until September 1, 1951, the government insured only the first $4,000 of any VA mortgage.

Nearly all veterans of World War II, and the Korean and Vietnam wars were subsequently entitled to $12,500 of VA mortgage eligibility. If you used only $4,000 or $7,500 of that eligibility, you qualify for another VA mortgage with the government insuring your mortgage-lender for the difference between $12,500 and either $4,000 or $7,500, whichever you have already used up in a previous VA mortgage.

You may also be eligible for a second or even a third VA mortgage if you had a VA mortgage that was closed out for a "compelling reason." That would include, for example, a house you bought with a VA mortgage and had to sell, washing out the mortgage, because your job required moving to another city or you went back into the service. The details on this and whether you qualify for a VA mortgage today, even though you had one in the past, can get complicated. To clear them up, consult a mortgage man in your nearest VA office.

FHA Mortgages

The FHA mortgage program is, in effect, a GI Bill of Rights for all home-buyers. It can enable any veteran or nonveteran to buy a house with a low down payment, and it contains other good features. Remember, though, that the Federal Housing Administration neither lends money to buy a house nor builds houses nor furnishes house plans. You get an FHA mortgage from FHA-approved mortgage lenders, with the FHA sweetening the loan by insuring the lender against loss if the buyer defaults. Hence the term *FHA-insured mortgage*. Here are some of the advantages of an FHA mortgage:

(1) *Its low down-payment scale* permits you to buy a house with as little as 3 percent down in cash—for example, $450 for a $15,000 house. The down payment rises in increments up to $5,000 (14.3 percent) for a $35,000 house. This often means you can build or buy a house with considerably less cash than

ordinarily needed with a conventional (nongovernment) mortgage. Conventional financing usually requires at least 10 percent down for a low-priced new house and usually up to 20 or 25 percent for higher-priced houses and for many used houses. Because FHA's low down-payment scale applies to old as well as to new houses, an FHA mortgage can therefore be particularly attractive for buying an old house.

(2) *Long repayment terms*—usually up to thirty years to repay —mean low monthly mortgage payments. It can ease the home-ownership burden considerably for people with tight budgets. In some special cases the term can be extended to thirty-five years, with even lower monthly payments. Of course, you will pay more interest over the long term, but you will be ahead of the game compared with renting a house. The FHA also gives you a prepayment privilege, allowing you to repay a little extra on your mortgage when you accumulate extra cash. That lets you pay off the mortgage earlier than otherwise, thus reducing your total interest charges.

(3) *Built-in construction safeguards* protect you in an FHA home loan. A new house approved for an FHA mortgage must meet minimum construction standards, and the builder must give you a one-year warranty on the house. If anything goes wrong, the builder must go back and make amends, or else he is blacklisted by the FHA. He will no longer be allowed to sell houses with FHA mortgages. But don't expect the builder to correct wear-and-tear damage or damage caused by poor maintenance or home-owner neglect. He doesn't have to go that far.

If a serious structural defect shows up and the builder is unwilling or unable to repair it, or if he has gone out of business, the FHA can step in and pay for the necessary corrective work, whether it costs $100, $1,000, or $10,000. You get this valuable new protection for up to four years after a new house is built and sold.

The four-year protection against serious defects in a new house is, in fact, a revolutionary advance in safeguards for the home-buyer (even though indications so far are that the FHA people are dragging their feet on enforcing it). It applies to new houses approved for FHA mortgages on or after September 2,

1964, though not to all new houses. The new house you buy must be one that "was approved by FHA for a mortgage prior to the beginning of construction and inspected by FHA or VA during construction." Some new houses are not okayed for FHA financing until after they have been started. Buy one of these, and you don't get the four-year protection. To play safe, check with the FHA beforehand to determine if the house qualifies for the four-year protection. It should also be specified in your sales contract with the builder.

A secondhand house bought with an FHA mortgage is not ordinarily covered by the new major-defect protection. An FHA appraiser checks the house beforehand, and FHA generally requires that any serious defects must be corrected before it will okay a mortgage. But if a defect shows up later, neither FHA nor anybody else can help you.

The one exception to this rule is that the FHA major-defects protection will cover you if your house was originally built and sold as a new FHA house on or after September 2, 1964, and meets the other FHA requirements noted above. You are then covered for four years after the house was originally *built*.

If you buy a house with a VA or any other kind of mortgage, it's up to the builder to correct defects. The four-year protection so far is exclusive with FHA. It may, however, eventually be extended to new houses with VA mortgages, possibly by the time you read this. Keep in mind that there is no such thing as an "FHA-approved" house in the sense that FHA puts on a stamp of approval. FHA simply requires that houses with FHA-insured mortgages conform to certain minimum construction standards.

(4) *FHA's special advantages for veterans and servicemen.* A veteran can obtain an FHA mortgage with a lower down payment than a nonveteran can—as low as $200 down for a $15,000 house rather than $450—though these down-payment figures may be changed at any time. The down-payment schedule for higher-priced houses is proportionately less. There are other features for veterans that are too lengthy (and too full of gobbledy-gook) to include here. Because the terms are continually subject to change, we suggest you write for them, together with details about regular FHA mortgages, to the Federal Housing Admin-

istration, Washington, D.C. 20411, or check with the nearest
FHA office.

FHA mortgages for servicemen are designed to enable a person
in military service with at least two years of active duty to buy a
house when he would otherwise be unable to do so while on active
duty. The terms (down payment, etc.) are much like the regular
terms for an FHA home loan, except that while on active duty a
soldier saves the ½ of 1 percent insurance-premium charge added
to regular FHA loans. The Defense Department pays that charge
for him each month. It means a saving of $2 to $3 a month, more
or less, depending on the mortgage. To qualify, a serviceman
must furnish the FHA with a Certificate of Eligibility (Form
DD 802) obtained from his commanding officer.

There is, however, a potential snare to avoid before you try for
an FHA serviceman's mortgage. It can indeed make easy buying
a house where you are stationed, particularly if it's tough to get a
place to rent. But if you are transferred and can't sell the house,
you are still liable for the mortgage. You risk a financial loss if,
for example, you are forced to unload the house at a price below
its worth. Besides, it ordinarily does not pay to buy a house unless
you live in it for at least three to four years. It takes that long to
build up enough equity in a house to make it better financially
than renting. That goes for all people, not just servicemen, and
regardless of whether you buy a house with or without an FHA
mortgage.

Avoid Paying "Points" for FHA and VA Mortgages

A mortgage-lender may charge a special fee called points when
he gives an FHA or VA mortgage. This can cost you extra money.
One point means 1 percent of the mortgage. The charge is de-
ducted from the loan before it is made. The number of points
varies from time to time according to the supply of mortgage
money. It can range from one point up to ten, sometimes more,
thus that much off the mortgage.

Builders also can take it on the chin during periods of tight
money as a result of points. Say, for example, a builder sells a
house with a $20,000 mortgage at a time when lenders are

charging six points. Instead of getting the full $20,000 from the lender when the house is sold, the builder gets only $18,800. That's $1,200 less (6 percent of $20,000) off the top of the mortgage amount. It is illegal, however, for the buyer to pay the points fee on an FHA or VA mortgage, so the builder is forced to absorb it to sell his houses.

As a buyer you should watch out for two things if points are involved when you buy. First, if a builder must pay an excessive points charge to get the VA or FHA mortgage you want, he may skimp on the house. Second, some builders or owners of used houses try to get the buyer to pay the points charge, as illustrated by the case of a young veteran we'll call Don Parsons, who was buying a $25,000 house.

It required a $2,500 down payment, and the rest of the purchase price was to be covered with a $22,500 mortgage. The real-estate agent handling the deal told Parsons that unfortunately a GI mortgage could be arranged only at the cost of a four-point fee. That was $900 (4 percent of $22,500). In other words, Parsons would have to pay $900 extra to the seller, in cash, to get the mortgage. A GI mortgage was essential for Don, because a conventional mortgage would require a considerably larger down payment as well as a higher interest rate.

The agent explained: "That's the way things are these days. Practically nobody is giving GI or FHA mortgages at face value. The interest rates are fixed by law at a lower rate than banks can get on conventional mortgages. We're in a tight-money situation today. The banks have all the takers they want for conventional mortgages. They are giving GI or FHA mortgages today only if they get four points."

Parsons was asked to pay the $900 in cash under the table, because the VA and the FHA make it illegal for the buyer to pay it. The seller may pay it, and that's perfectly legal, and everybody would be satisfied, except the seller, in this case. The seller did not want to because it would come out of the $25,000 he got for the house. He did not relish a $900 loss on the sale.

Suppose you are asked to pay points in addition to the sales price of a house. Your alternatives are clear. You can refuse and

let the seller pay (which is legal), you can back out of the deal,
or you can try for a conventional mortgage.

Conventional Mortgages

Conventional mortgages make up the majority of house mortgages. They are made by private lenders, including most banks,
savings and loan associations (also called building and loan associations), insurance companies, and mortgage brokers. You can
also get a conventional mortgage from a rich uncle, a business as-
sociate, or the seller of the house you're buying. It's called a
conventional mortgage mainly to distinguish it from government-
insured VA and FHA mortgages. Many of the same lenders, inci-
dentally, will also give VA and FHA home loans.

The biggest advantage of a conventional mortgage is the ease
of obtaining one. You can almost always get one simply by ap-
plying to one or more of the usual sources noted above. However,
there is no uniformity necessarily among conventional mortgages.
The interest rate you must pay is usually a little higher than the
going rate for FHA and VA mortgages, but it also can vary a
little from one lender to another. The down payment required,
maximum repayment period, other clauses in the mortgage loan,
and closing-cost charges can vary from one lender to another.

That brings up again the high importance of shopping for a
mortgage. Try all the lenders around. Besides checking the closing
costs charged by each, check on the maximum mortgage offered
and such things as interest rates. While you're at it, you can also
determine who offers FHA and, if you qualify, VA mortgages.

Desirable Mortgage Features

Don't be blinded by a low interest rate alone. Other important
features of a mortgage also count a lot, such as the presence or
omission of the following special features:

A *prepayment clause* permits you to pay off part or all of your
mortgage earlier than the schedule calls for. It lets you sharply
reduce your overall interest charges as well as the period of time

required to pay off the mortgage. It can also save you money if you sell the house before the mortgage is paid off.

Not all mortgage-lenders let you prepay, however, and some charge a penalty fee if you do. The FHA permits you to prepay up to 15 percent of your mortgage balance in any year up to the tenth year of the mortgage with no prepayment charge; after that you can prepay any sum with no penalty. The VA lets you prepay any amount any time. The prepayment clause is also the pleasant consolation for the home-buyer who, strapped financially in the beginning, must strive for the absolutely lowest monthly payments when he buys a house, though he is bothered by the many years required to pay off the loan. Later he can prepay on the loan as he gets ahead financially, thereby cutting down the number of years left to pay off the loan.

An *open-end clause* lets you refinance your mortgage quickly, easily, and cheaply, because there's no new set of stiff closing costs. Need a few thousand dollars or so? Just tell your mortgage-lender, sign a few papers, and you get it. But unlike a quick divorce, there's nothing questionable about it. You can borrow up to as much money as you've paid off on the mortgage and sometimes at the same interest rate as the mortgage. The refinancing charge is usually no more than $100 to $150. The mortgage is simply extended to let you pay off the additional loan. It's the answer to the need for money later to improve or expand a house, to send a child to college, to pay a big medical bill, or to satisfy any other money need.

An *appliance-and-household-items clause* lets you include the cost of major appliances and other big-ticket items (such as wall-to-wall carpeting) in the mortgage. This can be a boon especially when you buy a new house. You can finance the items at a low interest rate, compared with financing them with a short-term high-interest regular installment loan.

It can also cost you money, however, in higher total interest over the long term. That's the case if you pay off the appliances over the full period of the mortgage. You can eat your cake and have it, too, by taking advantage of a prepayment clause in your mortgage to pay off that part of the home loan that went for appliances and other such items as you can afford to.

Typical Mortgage Payments

Here are the monthly payments required for conventional mortgages at various interest rates:

Monthly Payments for a 25-Year Home Mortgage

Mortgage loan	25-year mortgage		
	6%	7%	8%
$ 1,000	$ 6.45	$ 7.07	$ 7.72
2,000	12.89	14.14	15.44
3,000	19.33	21.21	23.16
4,000	25.78	28.28	30.88
5,000	32.22	35.34	38.60
10,000	64.44	70.68	77.19
15,000	96.65	106.02	115.78
20,000	128.87	141.36	154.37

Monthly payments for other mortgages at the same interest rate can be easily computed. For example, monthly payments for a $25,000 mortgage at 7 percent are equal to those for a $20,000 mortgage ($141.36) plus those for a $5,000 mortgage ($35.34), or $176.70. The payments for a $30,000 mortgage will be ten times those for a $3,000 mortgage; for a $40,000 mortgage ten times those for a $4,000 mortgage; and so on. Monthly payments for twenty-year mortgages will be greater than those for twenty-five years, and payments for a thirty-year mortgage will be less. Exact payment figures for any mortgage not ascertainable from this table should be available from a bank or other mortgage-lender from whom you may obtain a mortgage.

Payments for a Veterans Administration mortgage at the same interest rate are the same as above. Payments for FHA mortgages at the same interest rates are slightly higher than those in the table, because the FHA adds a small "premium" charge (which is sometimes refundable afterward).

How Much Cash Down Payment Is Best?

So far we've emphasized the lowest down payment permissible on different mortgages, the minimum amount of cash required to buy a house. You may be able to pay more. You may feel you should on the theory that it is the financially correct thing to do. After all, the more money you pay in cash for a house, the less the mortgage loan and the more you save on interest charges.

A large down payment also may get you a lower interest rate, compared with the interest charged on the maximum mortgage for the same house. The lender may cut the interest rate by ¼ or even ½ of 1 percent if you make a large down payment. The proponents of a large down payment also state that it's a good thing to make a big investment in your house; it adds to one's credit rating, making you financially stalwart—and besides, buying a house is one of the best investments a person can make.

But there's another side to the story. A small down payment can make sense, too. Don't hasten to put all your spare cash into the down payment. Weigh the pros and cons first. A small down payment lets you keep cash in reserve for the expenses you may face after buying the house. Remember that money owed on a mortgage can be repaid at by far the lowest interest rate of virtually any consumer loan. It's much cheaper than later finding yourself in a bind and being forced to borrow with an installment loan at two to three times the interest rate.

Conserving your cash can mean other benefits, too. The larger your mortgage, the more you may save on income taxes, since mortgage-interest payments are tax-deductible. There are the possible higher earnings on your capital if it is invested elsewhere than in your house. And sometimes a low down payment can make it easier to sell your house to a buyer who takes over the mortgage. The larger your mortgage balance at the time, the less cash a buyer needs to buy the house. So don't feel compelled to put every last dollar into the down payment of a house. For some it may be the financially proper thing to do. For you the opposite may make more sense.

Second Mortgages

By and large, a second mortgage should be approached with the caution usually reserved for a king cobra. Watch out. Both the VA and FHA turn thumbs down on them, not permitting them with one of their first mortgages, because second mortgages usually carry stiff interest charges and must be repaid in a short period, such as five years. That can put an intolerable financial burden on a family, since it must be repaid at the same time you're paying off the first mortgage.

A second mortgage may be suggested when the buyer of a house lacks the cash needed for a large down payment. Say you want to buy a $35,000 house, but the top mortgage obtainable is $24,000. You must make up the difference with $11,000 in cash, but you can put down only $6,000. That leaves $5,000 to be made up, and the buyer suggests you take a second mortgage loan for it. At first glance, it may seem the simple thing to do, but when you see the payments required to pay it back plus possible hooks in the loan, it can take on an entirely different color. Besides, it implies that the house is overpriced. Otherwise a larger mortgage might be obtainable.

There are also times, to be sure, when a second mortgage can make sense. But be sure of what you're doing before you go ahead, and be sure that you will be able to pay it off at the same time you pay off the first mortgage.

If you can't get a satisfactory mortgage or lack the money for the down payment, all is not necessarily lost. Some builders and some homeowners will let you rent the house, with part or all of the rent money contributing to the eventual down payment. You get an option to buy after paying a certain rent. A variety of other sales-lease and land-contract arrangements can also be made. Some are perfectly aboveboard; others could hurt you badly.

Before signing such a contract, have a lawyer check it. Get your own lawyer, choosing one who really knows real-estate contracts. Don't use the seller's lawyer just because you are told you'll save money on the fee. Those are famous last words.

Should You Take Over an Existing Mortgage on a House?

The owner of a house for sale suggests that you take over his mortgage. It may or may not be a good idea. It can save you money if it carries a lower interest rate than currently available. Say he has a 6 percent mortgage with eighteen years to run, and today the best you can get is a 7¼ percent loan. Over the remaining years of the mortgage, you could save several thousand dollars in interest charges, compared to the higher-cost mortgage. And taking over a mortgage can mean reduced closing costs.

On the other hand, assuming a seller's mortgage usually means a high down payment. The seller must get back the money he has paid off on the house. The extra down payment required represents capital that you might invest elsewhere to better advantage.

If you are selling your house, letting a buyer take over your mortgage is still another matter. It can be deadly if done without thought. It may help you sell your house at a better price, but you must be sure liability for the mortgage is passed on to the buyer. Otherwise the original mortgagor (you) will be liable if the buyer defaults. To protect yourself, obtain a release of liability from the buyer. *Insist that the mortgage be rewritten in the buyer's name.* You'll also need written permission from the original mortgage-lender and from the FHA or VA if they are involved.

Some buyers will refuse. Then don't go ahead unless you take the following precautions. First, get a credit check on the buyer. Stop at once if he is a shaky credit risk. Second, have the buyer sign a bond and warrant. This makes him fully liable and enables the lender to force the sale of his other assets if he defaults on the loan. You will then be personally liable only for the amount that is left unpaid. Third, insist on an agreement prohibiting the buyer from transferring the mortgage to anybody else should he sell the house before the mortgage is paid off. Fourth, the sales-agreement clause should bind the buyer to keep the house adequately insured and properly maintained.

Some sellers, to be sure, have made out well by regaining their house after a buyer has defaulted. But this usually entails considerable legal wrangling, and you may not get the house back for as long as a year or two after default, the period required in some states.

Actually, the safeguards recommended above are by no means unreasonable. They are, in effect, little more than is required when you take out a first mortgage. If you are buying a house, you, too, could give the seller the same written assurances. You would end up being solely liable for the mortgage. Anything wrong with that?

The Vanishing Builder

There is no surer way to get stuck with a new house with small or big problems than to buy it from one of the vanishing-builder breed. The man may strike you as completely trustworthy, and indeed sometimes he is—at least in the beginning. The house not only may be spanking new but may look as solidly constructed as any. It may even be a house approved by the FHA or the VA.

But when something goes wrong with it, the builder is no longer around. It may be a small thing—a warped door, sticky windows, or a busted faucet—or it may be something really serious, such as chronic flooding of the basement, a defective furnace, or a bum septic tank (and the plumbing stops working).

Whatever it is, your calls for help go unanswered, or you may find, to your surprise and distress, that there's no phone listing for him. He may never have had one, in fact.

He simply may be unable or unwilling to make repairs. He

California house, let down by a buckled foundation and a vanishing builder, had to be jacked up to permit installation of sound underpinnings. The owner paid. (*Ernest Reshovsky*)

may have gone out of business or left town quietly. Whatever the reason, he has vanished as far as you are concerned. You are left high and dry (and sometimes not so dry).

Analyze all the instances in which home-buyers have been stuck with bad houses, and in nearly every one you'll find involved one form or another of the vanishing builder. The pattern becomes clear, and so does the obvious conclusion: There is no surer way of getting a good house than to avoid the vanishing builder. In short: *Deal only with a reputable builder*. That may smack of the stock advice offered freely and frequently by everyone who gives advice on home-buying. But it's easier said than done when you buy a house.

Before we get into how to avoid the vanishing-builder trap, be assured that the picture is not all black. It should be emphatically said that by no means are most builders gyps, chiselers, or con men. I know of home-builders with high principles who are

Phi Beta Kappa graduates of Harvard and Yale. I personally know a good many with established records for building good houses. That kind of builder need not take a back seat to any businessman in terms of professional ability, pride in his craft, and the quality of his product.

There is also a gray area where builders, just like people in other professions and fields of business, sometimes skirt the edges of morality. Their houses may not be as honestly built and soundly constructed as top standards would call for, but they are not necessarily shoddy or jerry-built. There are also builders with honest intentions whose knowledge of construction and whose ability to perform unhappily fall short of those intentions.

Then there is the vanishing builder, the worst of the bunch. Spokesmen for the building industry contend that he makes up a tiny minority of all builders, though the evidence suggests otherwise. Even if his number is not great, unfortunately his breed puts up a disproportionately large number of bad houses.

The Wake of the Vanishing Builder

A few examples should be cited together with a little detail about the vanishing builder. This can help you establish the profile of the kind of builder to avoid.

Item: A family we'll call Johnson and ten other families bought $30,000 to $35,000 houses a few years ago in a development we'll call Paradise Knolls. It's in a distant suburb of New York, a site of great natural beauty with the blue-gray Ramapo Mountains in resplendent view to the west.

After moving in, the Johnsons and their fellow neighbors had a series of troubles due to poor drainage. Their septic-tank system constantly overflowed. "The sewage smell is awful," Mrs. Johnson told a newspaperman. She also said, "Water has seriously damaged our tile flooring, the wallboard is mildewing, and water comes into the house so often we have all we can do to get rid of it. We brought in thirty-two truckloads of earth to divert the water . . . it only comes in slower. The State Supreme Court granted us a three-thousand-dollar judgment against the builder, but we can't collect."

Other families in Paradise Knolls must cope with sickening

pools of smelly water in their basements, despite pumps going twenty-four hours a day to get rid of the water. Pools of stagnant water overflow lawns and driveways. The embattled families tried for eighteen months to get the builder to remedy their problems, but to no avail. The local Health Department is sympathetic but can do nothing. Other families also obtained court judgments against the builder but can't collect either.

The houses were built and sold by a builder from Long Island, another part of the state. He was apparently unable or unwilling to correct the problems. In effect, the builder has vanished (though it is said that he is building elsewhere under a different company name).

Item: In Ventura, California, an epidemic of cracking floors, broken pipes, and buckling foundations hit the buyers of 249 houses in a tract called Weathersfield. It was like an earthquake. A survey by the Chamber of Commerce showed that 159 of the houses were defective. Some were virtually beyond repair and had to be abandoned. Some families could salvage their homes only by having them jacked up at a cost of over $2,000 each so that a new concrete floor could be poured underneath. The owners paid this bill themselves, since the builder had "vanished."

Item: A couple put a $600 deposit on a house to be built in a Chicago suburb. Nothing happened for months. The couple finally realized their house would not be built and tried to get their deposit back, but they were out of luck. This was no fly-by-night building firm. It was a subsidiary of the Dover Construction Company, a big outfit at the time with seventeen different building operations in four midwestern states.

The couple filed suit against Dover but did not get anywhere. The reason soon became clear. The Dover people had filed a petition for debt adjustment and reorganization under Chapter II of the Bankruptcy Act in the U.S. District Court in Chicago. It listed some $6,000,000 in debts to 288 creditors which it could not pay. There was little chance of the couple's getting its money back, and no telling how many other buyers of Dover's houses in the Midwest had also lost their money.

Lost deposits on new houses constitute a particularly cruel thing that happens to many people who can ill afford it. I know of eight families who each lost over $5,000 in deposits on houses that were started but then abandoned half finished. To pile hurt upon hurt, the bank financing the houses for the vanishing builder turned around and sued each buyer for the money *it* had lost on the houses!

How Do Such Things Happen?

How could such builders get away with it? And doesn't the home-buyer have any recourse?

One of the biggest culprits is the floating vanishing builder, who generally operates in a large metropolitan area. Sometimes he hastily puts together a building operation staked by men who latch on to a chunk of land in order to make a killing in housing. They often know little or nothing about house construction. Often they're not even builders. They just have some land and some capital and a burning desire to make a quick profit.

Such firms generally care little about the quality of the houses being put up. They aim for fast construction and even faster sales. When the last house is finished and sold, the profits are divided up, and the corporation is disbanded. If anything goes wrong with the houses, the "builder" can easily duck his responsibility even if the homeowners haul him into court.

A Long Island, New York, home-buyer, for example, won a hands-down $5,200 judgment against his builder for repairs that the builder refused to make, but he (the buyer) collected nary a dime. The builder had cannily drained his corporate till of all its assets. This is the widespread ploy known as corporation folding. The aggrieved homeowner was not only stymied but understandably enraged every morning when he could see the very same builder throwing up new houses across the road with a new corporation that was not legally liable to him or to any other buyer of the builder's previous houses.

That should alert you to the first ominous portent of potential trouble. When houses in a new development are being put up by a builder with a new corporation, often the corporation has been formed just to develop a single group of houses. Be on guard even if the builder proudly tells you about other houses he has

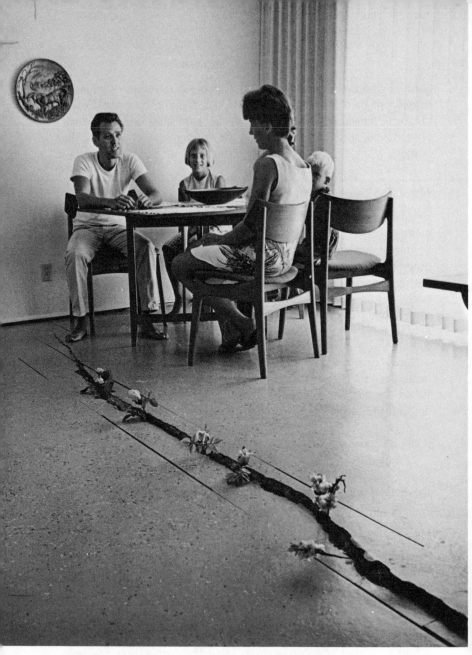

What do you do when your house starts cracking up and the builder doesn't do anything about it? This California family decorated a crack in the dining-room floor with plastic flowers. (*Ernest Reshovsky*)

built; you may find that they were built under other corporate names.

An established professional builder doesn't form new corporations all the time. He sticks with one company name. This is not necessarily to say that every new corporation putting up houses should be suspected. You can't necessarily tell for sure. But because it is a major identifying mark of the vanishing builder, the new corporation builder should be viewed with a strong dose of skepticism. It could be your first clue that all is not right.

The vanishing builder usually has little or no fear of the law. The law, in fact, has by and large proved ineffectual with such builders. That means most district attorneys, other public officials or agencies (such as your attorney general), the FHA, the VA, and anybody else you might think could help. All of these people are by law concerned only with criminal violations. To nail a recalcitrant builder, they need clear evidence of fraud. This is often tough to get, or so they say. As a result, the typical district attorney

Crumbling houses and shattered dreams: One-family row houses are literally cracking up because of being built improperly on former swampland. The builders refused to make repairs and later filed bankruptcy papers. (*The New York Times*)

may listen to your woes sympathetically but in the end give you the brush-off. He's dreadfully sorry, he will say, but it's so darned hard to prove fraud. Patting you on the back in consolation as he leads you to the door, he'll say that you'll have to hire a lawyer and take the case to civil court. However, help for home-buyers should come soon, since consumer advocates (like Ralph Nader) will almost certainly turn their attention to housing.

Cracking Down on Gyp Builders

It is because of the glaring indifference shown by many law-enforcement people that some builders have continued to build inferior houses. If officials would get tough, there would be far fewer abuses in home construction. This is shown by the results of an unprecedented crackdown by an untypical district attorney in an outlying residential section of Brooklyn. The story of what happened there may be straying a bit off the subject of this chapter, but nonetheless it should be told, since it sheds light on the national problem and what could be done about it.

Literally hundreds of houses, priced from $25,000 to $50,000, began cracking at the seams. Foundation walls were slowly sinking into the poorly filled land. In addition, the builders had promised paved streets, but left dirt roads that were muddy quagmires after every rain. Raw sewage backed up into the house basements in floodlike quantities following rain: The house drainpipes had been hooked up to the street lines in a flagrantly illegal manner.

The home-buyers complained to a series of city officials to no avail. In desperation they went to Brooklyn District Attorney Ed Silver (later made a judge), who was appalled by what he heard. Silver and his staff launched an investigation. It took nearly three years to get the evidence needed to prosecute. The upshot of the investigation was the conviction of one of the builders, Richard Powell and his Donven Realty Corporation, on a charge of first-degree grand larceny. Though Powell's conviction was later overturned in a higher court, his case made it clear to other builders that the district attorney meant business. Five other builders were indicted. A city plumbing inspector was convicted of taking bribes. Eight FHA inspectors and a VA construction official were also indicted on bribery charges brought by the federal government.

An interesting comment: "These things don't happen in a vacuum," we were told by Assistant District Attorney Irving Seidman, who was instrumental in the investigation. "Shoddy construction goes hand in hand with corrupt inspectors," he says. The investigation also prompted a stream of inquiries from DA's in other cities.

Probably the most significant outgrowth of the investigation was the "cleansing effect on other builders," in the words of Aaron Koota, then chief of the Brooklyn Rackets Bureau, who later became Brooklyn District Attorney. He said, "After our indictment, it was amazing how fast the builders made repairs." The outlying area where the epidemic of faulty houses and muddy streets prevailed has by and large become an attractive residential area. Many of the builders (though not all) went back and came to terms with the homeowners, repairing defects and putting in paved streets and sidewalks. Following the repairs, house values there shot up as much as 50 percent. A happy ending, but it took strong help from a persevering district attorney's staff.

What about FHA and VA Controls?

What help can you expect if something goes wrong with a house you buy with an FHA or VA mortgage? Both agencies will put pressure on the builder to correct defects that show up during the first year of ownership, the period covered by the usual warranty. This often produces results, for if the builder does not follow through, he will be, in effect, blacklisted by both agencies. He could no longer build and sell houses with VA or FHA mortgages. But the government can't force him to make repairs. Some builders refuse, apparently unconcerned about a government blacklisting. They can still build and sell houses with conventional mortgages.

If, however, you buy a house now with an FHA mortgage and the builder refuses to make repairs, you can get redress under the FHA's four-year major-defect guarantee reported in Chapter 3.

This major-defect protection was made into a law by Congress following a *Saturday Evening Post* magazine article, "Why New Houses Cost Too Much," which pointed up causes of poorly built houses as well as reasons for high costs.

There was an interesting postscript to the article after the National Association of Home Builders, the powerful national trade association of home-builders, lambasted it as "sensational" journalism full of half-truths. The president of the NAHB at the time, a big builder named W. Evans Buchanan, wrote the *Post* a fiery letter saying, among other things, that he was " . . . outraged at the distorted picture that emerged from your article." He said that the instances of faulty construction reported in the article represented a tiny number of isolated cases, and by far the overwhelming majority of builders were honest, upright men who built houses of outstanding quality.

A condensed version of Mr. Buchanan's letter ran in the "Letters" column of a subsequent issue of the *Post*. A few days later the *Post* received a letter (never published) from a lawyer prompted by Buchanan's "anguished response" to the article. The lawyer wrote that his personal experience fully bore out the content of the article. He had recently bought a house containing a multitude of defects like those mentioned in the article, plus others. What's more, he added, "my home was built by W. Evans Buchanan Co.!" (The author of this book can report that story because he was also the author of the *Post* housing article.)

Other Reasons for Problem Builders

Building houses is an exceedingly tough business. It holds pitfalls for builders as well as for buyers. This brings on hardships that are sometimes beyond the builder's ability to cope with. Some builders are betrayed by chiseling subcontractors or by callous workmen who mess up a house and cover up the shoddy workmanship. There is also the time-consuming difficulty of finding good subcontractors and then getting them to show up at the proper time. Many builders also face an incredible hodgepodge of local regulations and arbitrary building-code demands, which can make it impossible to build efficiently. And then there are the exasperating obstacles put in the builder's path by some political bureaucrats who run things with dictatorial hands from power posts in municipal building departments. That includes some building inspectors whose performance leaves much to be desired, as well as those who reportedly shake down builders.

As a result of such difficulties, the builder's lot is not easy. A hard-pressed builder can find himself in quite a jam, much of it not his own doing. No wonder then that some will throw up their hands in despair, saying there must be an easier way to make a living, and pull out, leaving their home-buyers holding the bag. We mention that side of the coin not only in fairness to those builders who strive hard to satisfy, but also to give a more rounded picture of the industry. Don't blame the builder for everything that goes wrong.

The builder's salesmen you encounter in a model house also rate a few words, since they can do you in (and also him). No matter how good the builder, one of his salesman can mislead you. Good salesmen are hard to come by. Even the best builders have little control over the wild promises and misstatements of *some* salesmen. They may be quick to tell you what a short distance it will be to the new school to be built or reassure you that the streets will be paved by a certain date. That's fine if such information is true. If it is vital information for you, though, it had better be double-checked.

The Hallmarks of the Good Builder

How do you spot a really good builder? Take the case of Andy Place, of Place & Sons, Inc., in South Bend, Indiana, whose firm has been building houses for decades and has won national awards for them. Among other things, Place guarantees that his houses can be completely heated and air-conditioned for no more than $150 a year operating cost, all told. In fact, total heating and cooling bills average closer to $125 a year per family, or less than $11 a month.

There's the firm of Fox and Jacobs in Dallas, Texas, long noted for the excellent community planning, among other things, of its new developments. There's Bob Schmitt Homes, of Berea, Ohio, headed by Schmitt, who has a national reputation in the industry for his technological innovations. There's Jon Aley, of

Clear evidence that a good builder did this new development: the trees, a pleasantly curved street, and a variety of house designs. This is part of Strathmore at Stony Brook, New York, development by Levitt & Sons, Inc. (*All About Houses*)

Jonathan Aley Company, who, though a relatively new builder, is noted for the outstanding quality of the custom houses he builds in the Westport-Weston area of Connecticut. And then there's Bill Levitt, noted largely for his Levittown communities, of the firm Levitt & Sons, Inc., started by his father in 1929. His houses are noted for an unusual number of special features (such as completely equipped kitchens and laundries), although his house sales prices are often substantially below the prices for comparable houses by other builders.

We could cite other builders of note who are the antithesis of the vanishing builder, but those just mentioned are sufficient to make an important point. Each one has always been in business with one company (no corporation folding), and in addition *each one uses his own name (or names) in his company name.* Those are two important hallmarks of a top-notch builder—an important thing to remember.

How to Check on a Builder

Most, though not necessarily all, reputable builders use their own names as part of their firm names. The builder's advertising, the signs around his houses, and his promotion material should play

This well-designed house bespeaks a superior builder. It's a two-story contemporary, especially designed for a New England setting and built by Emil Hanslin. Part of Hanslin's three-thousand-acre New Seabury development on Cape Cod, it was designed for him by the architectural firm of Royal Barry Wills Associates. (*Lisanti, Inc.*)

up his personal name. (Big companies like General Electric, Westinghouse, and Xerox pour millions into promoting their names.) Be wary, on the other hand, of the builder who promotes a particular tract name such as Happy Knolls or Sunshine Acres, with little or no emphasis on his name. He is one who should make you cautious. It could be the first sign of a vanishing builder.

Here is a checklist of other pointers for avoiding the vanishing builder and getting a good house.

• *Has the builder been established in business for some time?* The longer he has operated under the same name in the past, the longer you can expect him to be around in the future to take

This four-bedroom ranch house, originally priced at $21,500 in the mid-1960's, is another example of superior design of a builder tract house. It was designed by Florida architect Gene Leedy, A.I.A., for Levitt & Sons Rockledge development near Cape Kennedy, Florida.

care of possible problems. By and large, the well-established builder also has a permanent office headquarters in the area. He may live in one of his own houses nearby, perhaps the greatest accolade one could ask for. Building is his lifetime profession.

Check on these things by obtaining a financial report on the builder. It can usually be had for a few dollars through your local bank. The report will also give an indication of his credit rating. A low rating is clearly not good. Also ask the builder for credit references, including his bank. Check with each one. How long has he been in business? How reliable is he?

• *Does he have a record of building good houses?* A good builder will often have pictures of his houses on his office walls. He should tell you where you can see houses he has built and give you the names of at least half a dozen past buyers. See or call them; this is one of the best ways to find out how you are likely to fare.

• *Do local building material suppliers and subcontractors give the builder a good rating?* Talk to the builder's lumber dealer, plumbing supplier, and others. Also ask people in the local building department about him. These people know which builders cause trouble and which do not, though sometimes they are reluctant to criticize. If they can't say much good about a builder, watch out.

• *Is he a member of the Registered Builder program of the National Association of Home Builders?* If so, he may display the Registered Builder emblem of the NAHB. At last count, members of some sixty state and local builder groups have adopted Registered Builder programs, which means special safeguards for home-buyers. The first such program originated in Minneapolis and includes notable groups in other cities, such as Milwaukee, Wisconsin; Pittsburgh, Pennsylvania; and Charleston, South Carolina.

To display the Registered Builder emblem, a builder must pass certain professional and financial requirements set up by the local builder organization. He agrees to abide by certain rules and ethics in his dealings with the public. A special bonding program is also part of the program in some, though not all, of the Regis-

Even a small builder can achieve excellent results, as shown by this deceptively large New England saltbox done with authenticity as well as topflight construction. It is a custom house, speculatively built, by Westport, Connecticut, builder Jonathan Aley, designed for him by architect Thomas E. Bates. Note the direct and convenient access to the house by a private drive, an Aley trademark.

tered Builder groups. This, of course, is an additional safeguard for the home-buyer.

• *Call the Better Business Bureau about your builder.* If they can report nothing on him, it means no complaints have been received. Of course, this may not mean anything. If they report one or more complaints on his record, he should have satisfied the complaints. If he hasn't, it's a danger signal.

• *Does the builder have a listed telephone number?* It should not be a new number under the name of the development, such as for "Good Ole Rolling Acres" or "Sunset by the Sea." It should be in the name of the builder or his established firm. If not, watch out. Besides, if there's no permanent telephone listing, whom do you call with a problem after you buy the house?

A builder who scored high on the checklist is the very best assurance of your getting a well-built house. You can almost forget about peering into dark corners, checking the two-by-fours, and knocking on walls to see if they are solid. The house should be fairly well constructed at the very least. A good builder doesn't want call-backs or trouble any more than you do. They cost him money and time which eats into his overhead. But if something in the house doesn't work right, the odds are high that the good builder will take care of it. You will have little to worry about.

Conversely, you should look again, *carefully,* at the houses of a builder who scores low on the checklist. This is the stage at

This is the Registered Builder emblem of the National Association of Home Builders. Displayed by a builder, it means added protection for home-buyers.

which to tread slowly, even though the man's houses *seem* well built when you inspect them. It's because—and let's face it—most of us know little more about the intricacies of house construction than we know about laser beams. (And even if you happen to know about lasers, it doesn't make you a construction expert.)

Check out the builder first, rather than the construction of his houses, and you've made probably the biggest possible step forward toward getting a well-built house.

However, this refers chiefly to the construction quality of a house, as opposed to its intrinsic design. Design is something else again.

The No-Design
House

The no-design house lacks style, proportion, and beauty. But that's not all. There's more to design, or the lack of it, than mere good looks.

The no-design house is hard to live in and a nightmare to cope with and maintain. It's stuck on its lot with no thought given to taking advantage of the best view or the best exposure in relation to the overhead sun or the prevailing winds (heat and cold). Little or no thought is given to privacy for the occupants from passing traffic out front or from the eyes of neighbors on either side. And inside, the interior plan and room arrangements are often just as bad for meeting the needs of the humans who will live here.

That brings up the three main ingredients of a well-designed house: (1) good appearance, (2) a well-planned house-to-site relationship, and (3) good interior planning. The only way to avoid the no-design house and get a house that you will enjoy thoroughly and which will retain its resale value and be really satisfactory over the years is to understand these three essentials of good design and how to spot them when you shop for a house. We shall discuss the first two points here and the third in Chapter 6.

Good Appearance

Take a good look at a no-design house: You will often find that the facade is likely to be broken up with a mishmash of different materials put together like a banana split.

It may include blotches of stone or brick mixed in with two or three different kinds of wood siding. There is no coherence. You'll generally see walls jutting in or out here and there with many jogs and breaks. The roof lines are often broken up for no reason at all. This is supposed to add variety and interest but contributes to chaos instead. The doors and windows not only do not line up, but are often out of scale and character with the rest of the house. And here and there is hideous gingerbread adding to the clutter, like cheap jewelry piled over a flashy dress.

What is good appearance? One of the best answers is given in a book for professionals, *Construction Lending Guide: A Handbook of Homebuilding Design and Construction,* written by architects John L. Schmidt, Walter H. Lewis, and Harold Bennett Olin, for the United States Savings and Loan League. Here are some things the book has to say about good appearance.*

Exterior Appearance

Pleasing appearance is no accident. Careful study and organization are necessary to anticipate how a house will appear in finished form. The appreciation of a well-designed building is based on recognition and evaluation of the following points.

Proper Proportions

There are basic combinations of shape and mass that result in balanced building proportions. Portions of a building can be out of balance, just as a scale can be tilted. In traditional styling, the proportions of structures and the elements within the design have

* Copyright © 1966 by U. S. Savings and Loan League. Used by permission.

These three contemporary houses show how the wall material on a house can drastically affect appearance. (*Top photos: Techbuilt. Bottom: Lisanti, Inc.; illustration courtesy* Better Homes & Gardens, © *Meredith Corporation, 1964.*)

been refined through many years of study. Roof slopes, overhangs, window shapes, and sizes have all been carefully considered to fit with one another. In today's typical house design (in attempting to achieve the charm of traditional styling) familiar elements are often used without exercising proper care for achieving pleasing proportions.

Visual Organization

A house is a complex arrangement of parts and pieces. Success in exterior design rests in large part on the visual continuity of these elements, which should be related in shape, form and arrangement. Visual organization is the assembling of the parts and pieces with these relationships in mind.

Material Usage, Textures

Materials should be selected for uses appropriate to their capabilities. The elements of a house should be built of materials capable of performing satisfactorily, both initially and over the years.

The visual response aroused by various materials differs greatly. For example, the smooth, "cold" flatness of porcelain-enamel steel panels affects a viewer very differently from a rough, nubby stone wall of rich "warmth." The texture of materials is extremely important in the design of houses and in the selection of materials to be used.

In general, the number of textures selected should be held to a minimum; one type of masonry, one type of wood, or one siding texture, and one neutral "panel" surface per house. Contrasts can be used very successfully, just as a man can be well-dressed with a coat and trousers of different texture. The well-dressed man, however, and the well-dressed house do not wear many varying materials at the same time.

Scale

Scale is the relationship of design elements to the human being. One's visual sense depends in great part on scale relationships in judging distances, sizes and proportions. The size of a door in a house facade can be "in scale," that is, proportioned agreeably to the human being and to the rest of the house; or it can be "out of scale," that is, not properly related to the human figure, overpowering or diminutive in the entire design.

Simplicity and Restraint

To simplify is to refine. In housing, the simplest, most basic designs are the hardest to achieve but simple visual elements are the most pleasing. The attempt to make a house appear more expensive by cheap imitation of expensive items can be disastrous.

Scrollwork and carpentry bric-a-brac can result in design chaos. Such an approach is often based on using many unrelated elements in an effort to develop curb appeal. A storm door with a pelican scroll, a checkerboard garage door, slanted posts at the entrance-way, diamond-shaped windows and other parts and pieces having no design continuity detract from appearance and result in a modest house looking cheaper instead of costlier.

The most successful approach is one of restraint. Generally, the simply stated house design is the handsomest. Restraint and sophistication go hand in hand. And opulence and over-decoration are more often than not annoying and disturbing. The simplest designs are the most agreeable in the long run.

Color

Color is a highly potent factor in the design of a group of houses taken as a whole. In this respect, color coordination is a major way to strengthen that pleasing individuality from house to house, the objective of good subdivision design. Color is actually so powerful that it can make a cracker-box house look attractive or a generally well designed house look repulsive. It all depends on the skill with which color is used. When a large group of houses is involved, the over-all effect of color is a major concern. The cluttered, disorganized look of the average subdivision of low-to-moderate-priced houses (or even more expensive ones) is due largely to lack of color coordination. Clashing roofs, anemic body colors, misplaced accent colors—all these result from the short-sighted practice of giving the buyer too much latitude in selecting exterior color.

The All-Round Look

Unfortunately, most houses are designed like a Hollywood set. Some concern is evidenced over the appearance of the street facade, but often the side and rear elevations are totally neglected. A well-designed house, like a piece of sculpture, should be handsome when viewed from any vantage point.

A Few Words about Style

A well-known architect, Alden Dow, FAIA, puts it simply: "Style is a result, it can never be an objective. When style itself becomes the objective, nothing results but a copy."

What determines style? The shape and character, or style, of a house should be determined by the plan, the site, methods and materials of construction, and by the budget. A particular set of circumstances, worked upon by the design process, logically will lead to a particular set of building shapes or appearance. It might be correct to say that the well-designed house is styleless, since no forcing of the solution has been made by adapting it to the framework of a "traditional" scheme. Traditional styles are, of course, in predominance and undoubtedly will remain so for many years. But there are other styles to consider.

Here are four terms often discussed in describing other than traditional architecture: modern, modernistic, contemporary, and futuristic.

A *modern* house is one built of up-to-date materials: it has most of the current electrical and mechanical gadgetry in place and may exhibit itself as a simplified expression of any of the whole bag of traditional styles. It is harmless in design—not bad perhaps—but not great architecture.

A *modernistic* house is a poorly designed, "jazzy" modern house. Often it is an attempt at being unusual, generally is designed by a contractor or individual and is usually a collection of pieces (perhaps a flat roof or a butterfly roof, round windows, slanted posts, big "picture windows") with no integration of parts into a carefully studied design.

A *contemporary* house generally is one done by an architect and grows in its design from the consideration of beauty, function, and site. The market confuses good contemporary design with modernistic and fails to perceive the great difference between the two. Contemporary design is not faddish, or subject to being "in" today, "out" tomorrow. On the contrary, it's extremely rare, especially in lower-cost houses.

A *futuristic* house is somewhat experimental in nature. New products or methods may be tried or tested, and generally the futuristic house attempts to present an image of tomorrow's house. It may be, and usually is, a properly conceived design, but its importance on the market is inconsequential.

Poorly designed modernistic houses invariably will be penalized by the market, but an honestly conceived contemporary home, large or small, is of lasting value. Little research is necessary to recognize that a fine piece of architecture appreciates in value and appeal. Certainly the demand far exceeds the small supply.

The basic elements of good design are the same for all houses regardless of architectural style and era, as shown by these different houses. (*Bottom illustrations courtesy* Better Homes & Gardens, © *Meredith Corporation, 1966*)

Architectural Styles

A few additional words should be said about the sensitive subject of "style." What architectural style for you? You may prefer a traditional style, such as a Cape Cod or English Colonial house, or your taste may swing to the present in favor of an up-to-date contemporary house. Whatever you like, it's your prerogative. Stick to your guns.

However, words like "Colonial" and "contemporary" stir up fierce emotions, and one's sensitivities are easy to wound. Let's avoid that sort of thing and understand some of the basic facts and reasons surrounding the main kinds of American houses and how their designs developed. A look back can be instructive.

The Cape Cod House

Consider the Cape Cod house, a remarkable structure for its time and place. It was originally a tight little box with a massive chimney set in the dead center of the house. The chimney anchored the house against the shifting sands and howling winds of Cape Cod. The chimney was flanked by a small room on each side of the front door and in the rear by a large kitchen. That let each room of the house have its own fireplace built into the central chimney. The rooms were small because a fireplace could not heat much space.

The windows were small and shuttered (storm sash) to keep out windblown sand as well as the fierce winds of winter. The windows consisted of numerous small panes (lites) because the glass-blowing methods of the time could not turn out large panes. The house usually faced square to the south—not only to receive a maximum of warm sunshine in winter, but also to tell time. When the sun's rays came straight in a front window, hitting the marker on the floor, it was high noon.

It was the thriftiest sort of house, low and broad of beam, and measuring thirty-eight by twenty-nine feet, with ceilings only seven

The Jabez Wilder House, South Hingham, Massachusetts, was built about 1690. It is the kind of Cape Cod house with a bow roof, curved like the keel of a ship, built by a people familiar with shipbuilding techniques. The main house is almost as deep as it is wide; note how it hugs the ground. (*Charles Peterson, HABS, Library of Congress*)

feet high. The extra half-floor in the attic was originally left open as a dormitory. Straw pallets or trundle beds were put down for any number of children. As the family expanded—and some had as many as twenty-six offspring, according to old diaries—lean-tos were built on the side or back to sleep the overflow. The houses were never expanded upward. The large kitchen at the back, with its huge fireplace and built-in brick oven, was the natural center of activity for the family. In the summer, though, its stifling heat was too much, and a separate summer kitchen was often added at the back.

Over the years the basic design of the Cape Cod was changed and varied, and later it lost favor as Americans turned to other styles. But then later, much later, the Cape Cod reemerged as a popular house during the Depression days of the 1930's. Casting around for a thrifty and compact house to put up and sell, home-builders resurrected the Cape Cod, though not without serious modifications and changes not all to the good. That's why today you will see thousands on thousands of Cape Cods of one kind or another along the highways and byways of our country. They kept on building them following World War II, though by this time the fundamental reasons for an authentic or even modified Cape Cod were no longer valid.

The handsome, unadorned design of the Parson Capen House in Topsfield, Massachusetts, still stands out, though it was built in 1683. Wayne Andrews has called it "probably the finest remaining example of seventeenth-century American domestic architecture." (*Wayne Andrews*)

The Colonial and Later Houses

In the early days the Cape Cod was followed by five basic kinds of colonial houses: the English, French, Dutch, Spanish, and Southern Colonial. The early settlers tried to build houses that were as nearly as possible like their former homes in Europe but were forced to adapt them to a new climate, new materials, and different building conditions. The Southern colonists from England did better than their New England relatives, thanks to a milder climate and the availability of bricks and slave labor. They were better able to reflect the Georgian style of eighteenth-century England (as in Williamsburg, Virginia). The classical revival in England was later copied in the Southern plantation mansions with their two-story columns. The French settlers along the St. Lawrence River did not do well because of the lack of suitable materials. The French in New Orleans fared better, partly because the best architects were sent to Louisiana.

The New Amsterdam Dutch did splendidly, coming closest to duplicating their Holland dwellings, as testified by the fine old

The George Wythe House in Williamsburg, Virginia, built with native brick, is called a perfect example of Georgian Colonial architecture. It was built in 1755 for Wythe, the first professor of law at William and Mary College. (*Colonial Williamsburg*)

Dutch Colonials still standing along the Hudson River valley. The Spanish influence was short-lived in Florida but eventually survived in the Southwest, where it was well carried out with adobe, plaster, and other available materials.

In the nineteenth century the Gothic revival in England swept over to influence American architecture, and we had our hands full with Victorian houses of every kind and shape. Many of them, however, have no reason for surviving today other than providing the stuff for Charles Addams cartoons.

Then came the ranch house, an indigenous design, springing up from the sprawling ranch houses of the West. They were suitable for people who could afford a large house spread out luxuriously on cheap land. Today it's the most widely built kind of house. The ranch reached its acme of excellence in the prairie houses of Frank Lloyd Wright. Today we also have the Bauhaus school of modern architecture, illustrated at its best by exciting glass houses stemming from the work of architects Ludwig Mies van der Rohe and Philip Johnson. Some of their imitators, however, have cursed us with monstrous botched-up glass houses.

The Modern House

A good modern house makes plenty of sense today, largely because of central heating, a key influence on twentieth-century architecture. It lets us enjoy big rooms with large windows without discomfort. There's no longer any need for a fireplace in every room. With no longer a need for a coal bin, a basement is not essential (though it can be great for storage and utility purposes). And because of air conditioning, every room no longer requires two exposures for cross-ventilation.

In short, new materials and modern techniques can make a huge difference in the way houses are designed and built today, in contrast with the way houses were traditionally designed (and styled) in the past. For example, today, by using double panes, we can use large areas of glass, thus opening our houses to sun, light, and view without letting in cold and drafts.

That's the case, somewhat oversimplified, to be sure, for a good contemporary house design. You may still prefer a traditional house, assuming it gives you modern living advantages. But another characteristic of house design should be considered: the number of floor levels.

How Many Floor Levels?

There are one-story, one-and-a-half-story, two-story, and split-level houses. The one you choose can have an enormous influence on your day-to-day living convenience and pleasure. Knowing the pros and cons of each can also help you single out the best type for your family.

The One-Story House

The one-story house (ranch) excels for its glorious lack of stair climbing, a boon for the parents of small children as well as for elderly people. It's suitable for people with low, medium, or high incomes. It's the easiest kind of house to keep clean and maintain. This means not only reduced housekeeping labor and chores but also reduced maintenance and upkeep expenses. For example, the cost of painting the inside and outside of a one-story house

Frank Lloyd Wright's Robie House, built in Chicago in 1908, ranks as one of the most significant American houses of the twentieth century. It broke with the past and led the way to contemporary architecture in houses. (*Wayne Andrews*)

Falling Water, designed by Frank Lloyd Wright, was built in 1936 for E. J. Kaufmann, Bear Run, Pennsylvania. (*Wayne Andrews*)

runs 15 to 23 percent less than the cost of painting a two-story house, according to home-maintenance expert Henry Gilbert, president of the New York–based MacClean Service Company. (One of the reasons is the higher ladder cost for a two-story house.)

The one-story house allows the most flexible floor planning. It opens up the advantages of indoor-outdoor living (that much-used magazine phrase) to people in every room. Though it works best on flat land, it can be built on any terrain. Wherever it's built, though, it should hug the ground for aesthetic reasons and for safety. A one-story house looks awkward and ungainly when it sticks way up out of the ground and extra steps from the house to ground level are required. The fewer the steps, the better, particularly at night, when it's hard to see and accidents are more likely.

The main drawbacks of the one-story house have to do with its room zoning and construction. Because all rooms are side by side on one level, good separation between the living, working, and sleeping zones is essential. The spread-out plan also requires more land, which usually makes it more expensive, and the one-story house requires more roof and basement area than a multilevel house with the same overall interior space (though it's not so costly as you may think).

The One-and-a-Half-Story House

Fewer and fewer Cape Cods, the classic one-and-a-half-story American house, are bought these days because of the difficulty and expense of turning that raw unfinished attic into usable rooms. A full two-story house generally costs no more and usually less. Besides, the attic rooms in a Cape Cod, being under the roof, tend to be furnace-hot in summer and icy cold in winter. Special care in insulation and heating is essential to prevent these problems; but it is not always provided.

Dormer windows in the roof can violate the basic lines of the authentic Cape Cod and spoil the looks. If there's a basement under the house, the hole necessary for the stairwell can wreak havoc with the compact first-floor plan, where every square foot counts. In fact, recent research has shown that because of the space lost to the stairways up and down plus such things as the extra materials required for the steep roof, the Cape Cod is one of the costliest houses to build in terms of the net living space you get. So, sad to say, the charming old Cape Cod takes a back seat today to other, more economical and convenient kinds of houses.

The Two-Story House

A two-story house gives a feeling of large size and permanence and comes closest to our blurred notions of "Colonial." It leads the field in getting the most house on the least land. It's therefore supremely feasible on high-priced land or on a tight little lot. It offers natural separation (zoning) between the living activities downstairs and the bedrooms upstairs. It's also for people who have qualms about sleeping in bedrooms at ground level. Because it's compact, it can be somewhat easier to heat than a house on one spread-out floor level. And in summer the downstairs rooms tend to be cool, though the upstairs bedrooms can get quite hot if the attic isn't properly insulated and ventilated.

Its main drawback is the stair climbing, which makes house-cleaning tougher and puts great strain on parents of small children and on the elderly. It also puts restrictions on a family that likes to spend a lot of time outdoors during nice weather. Though the downstairs can be designed for easy access to outdoors, it's amazing how often you must come in and trudge up and down the stairs when you're doing things outdoors.

Ordinarily the two-story house should cost less to build than any other house, but not as much less as you might think. Extra room area must be provided to compensate for the space lost to the upstairs stairway, and what is saved on roofing area is partly if not entirely canceled out by the expense of getting materials to the second floor and roof.

The Split-Level House

The split-level is the house for a sloping lot; you can have at least two main floors with direct access to outdoors. There are side-to-side splits and front-to-back ones, depending on the slope and the best way to face the house; i.e., it can be built well on any slope. The different parts of the house can be zoned off from each other by putting them on different levels. Properly designed, a good split can look handsome and large, with the additional advantage of only a short stairway from one level to another.

Improperly designed, a split with numerous short stairways can be a decided pain in the neck (and legs). You find yourself going up and down far too often. The split is also complex, if not difficult, to build. This can run up its cost, especially if excessive bulldozing and grading are necessary or if retaining walls must be built. The lowest and highest levels demand especially good heating and insulation for comfort. The worst split-level houses—the no-design kind—are those that are stuck on a dead-level lot. That can make them look ungainly and awkward because they are unsuitable for a flat lot. The best ones, built on sloping land, look as if they grew out of a natural marriage between land and house.

Which Way Should Your House Face?

The siting of a house on its lot is the second vital ingredient of design. Ideally, the main living areas and the main windows should drink in the best view and should also face south. The best view

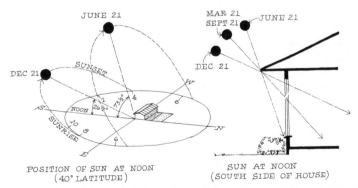

POSITION OF SUN AT NOON   SUN AT NOON
(40° LATITUDE)   (SOUTH SIDE OF HOUSE)

Diagram shows how the orbit of the overhead sun varies over the United States from the longest day in summer to the shortest day in winter. It also shows how a roof overhang on the south side of a house can shade a big window from hot sun in summer but let warm sunshine in the same window in winter. (*All About Houses*)

isn't always to the south, but we'll get to that in a moment. You can quickly tell if you will enjoy the best view simply by looking out the windows when you inspect a house. Is it a good vista? It may be a simple, serene view of grass and trees or a panoramic view of the Rocky Mountains or the Pacific Ocean. Or all you may see is asphalt street or a view of your neighbor's clothesline. A clothesline view is, of course, another mark of the no-design house.

The accompanying sun diagram shows why a southern exposure is ordinarily best: because of the predictable course changes of the overhead sun from season to season. In summer it rises in the *northeast* at morning and sets in the *northwest*. In winter, however, you'll see how the morning sun rises in the *southeast,* arcs across the sky at a much lower, more southerly direction, and sets in the *southwest.*

A southern exposure is therefore the only exposure that can let bright, warm sunshine flood into your house all winter long. This means not only that your house will be bright and delightfully pleasant with sunshine, but that your fuel bills may be lower. A southern exposure can also pay off in a cooler house in summer, because windows on the south are easy to shade from the hot sun—with deciduous shade trees, which obligingly lose their leaves in winter to let the sunshine through, or by deep roof over-hangings, which block out the overhead summer sun but let in the lower-angled southern sun in winter.

As for other exposures, a house that faces east or west gets the fierce brunt of hot sun in either the morning or the afternoon in summer (which is when you certainly don't want it) but much less sun during those cold days of winter. A house that faces north not only gets little sunshine in winter, but must bear the full bitter lash of cold winds in winter.

Sun versus View

Naturally the best view isn't always to the south. If it is not, a compromise is in order. A good middle ground is not impossible. Some big windows can be located to receive the view, whereas others face south to receive the winter sun. If you are buying a

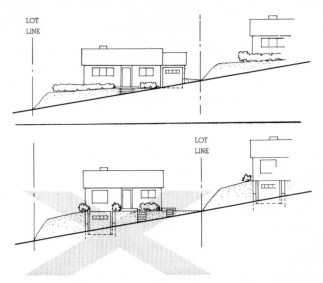

Right way to site a house on a sloping street (top) puts garage on same level, reducing steps and driveway slope as well as excavation cost. Wrong way (below) shows awkwardness that results when the opposite is done. (*All About Houses*)

Right way to site a house on sloping lot (left) puts first floor at ground level. Wrong way (right) raises house awkwardly above ground, making it look out of joint as well as adding extra steps. (*All About Houses*)

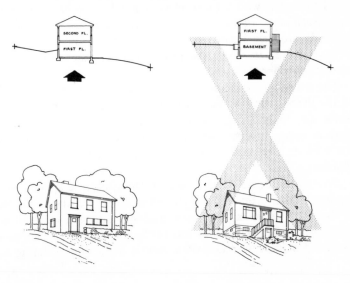

development house, ordinarily you have a choice of lots, so you can choose one that combines the best view with a southern exposure. You can also ask for design changes, if necessary, so the house is sited on its lot for the best orientation in relation to sun and view.

The House-Site Design

The house should be sited to give you the most use from your land. Mentally divide the lot into its three main areas: the public, the private, and the service zones. The public zone consists of the front lawn and that part of the grounds in public view. The private zone embraces that part, usually on the sides and/or rear of the house, reserved for your private outdoor use. The service zone includes the driveway, the walks, and the areas for trashcans, outdoor-equipment storage, and other such needs.

Ideally, a house should be set forward on its lot to give you the most amount of your land for private use in the rear, out of sight of neighbors and passing traffic. That also means a minimum of public zone in the front and thus minimal need for lawn-mowing and landscaping. You cut down on maintenance chores, leaving yourself more time to be out back, either at play with children or simply relaxing with a drink in your hand on your patio or terrace. Such outdoor living space can be easily created when the house is properly located on its lot. It may require help in the form of fences to screen the private part of your land from the view of outsiders.

The private zone of the lot should also have a good connection to the living zones of the house itself. The living areas inside the house should be located with convenient access to the patio or terrace, and vice versa. More on this in the next chapter, in which we take up the third vital ingredient of good design—interior planning.

To sum up the no-design house, it can usually be spotted within moments after you get out of your car to inspect a house. Is there too much lawn to mow and maintain in front, too little land for private, low-upkeep use in the back? Take a look at the overhead sun. How much of it gets into the house during cold weather? How much is kept out during warm weather? Does the house capture the best view? These are some of the functional things that you can measure by eye. And, of course, what about the overall style and design? Is it really well designed, or is it a no-design nothing house?

If there's one final test for a well-designed house, it's the presence of a good architect's signature on its plans. Unfortunately, only about one out of every four new houses today is designed by an architect, the biggest reason for no-design houses. Mention of architects also, to be sure, prompts skepticism in the minds of some people. They think of architects who are allegedly far more concerned with "aesthetics" than with designing a practical and economical house. This may well be true with some architects.

But by and large there are plenty of good architects around, and one is as essential for the planning of a really good house as a good engineer is essential for the planning of a bridge. If there's no architect, there's generally no design, in the true meaning of the word. Look for a good architect, and chances are you'll find a well-designed house, too.

The Garbled
Floor Plan

When you enter a house, ideally you should be able to go straight to any room without passing through a third room. If you must pass through a third room, it's a demerit. If you must cross the living room, it's one of the biggest sins. Think of the disruption it can cause when you're quietly entertaining guests and kids come barging through every time they enter or leave.

We know a woman whose biggest complaint about her house is its "Grand Central" living room. Located haphazardly in the center of the house, the living room must be used to get from the kitchen to the front door or to go upstairs. To get to the bathroom or to almost anywhere else in the house, she must also pass through the living room. "The living room congestion is as bad as Grand Central Station," she says.

We know another woman whose biggest complaint is her laundry, which is isolated in the basement. She must make repeated trips down and back—to start the wash, answer the buzzer, trans-

Excellent design of this rambling California house permits the owner's family to enjoy the outdoors to its fullest. Note clerestory in roof which lets outside sun and light pour directly into the center of the house. (*R. C. Lautman*)

fer clothes to the dryer, and so on. Never again will she have a house with a laundry away from her main post in the kitchen. It's too hard on her legs.

And we know of a woman who craves another house because her present house lacks a mud room. Particularly during bad weather, her children track in dust and dirt over freshly cleaned floors and rugs. A properly located mud room would permit the kids to get off their rubbers or boots before walking through the rest of the house. Actually, it's not necessarily the lack of a mud room per se that causes the trouble. It's a bad floor plan that requires children (and everybody else) entering the house to pass through various rooms before getting to an inside destination where they can shed dirty things and clean up.

These examples not only point up common troubles often encountered as a result of a garbled floor plan, but also illustrate the importance of good circulation in a house, which means the main traffic routes created by the basic floor plan. Good interior design also calls for proper zoning between each of the three main interior zones of a house—the living, sleeping, and working quarters—and it calls for logical and sensible planning of each room.

Clearly, the way to avoid the garbled-plan trap is to know a little about what constitutes good interior design. Start with the

Left: The plan for this modest ranch house is far from garbled. The garage also buffers the bedroom wing from the noise and eyes of street traffic in front. House is located in Oak Forest, Illinois, designed by architects Huebner and Henneberg. (*Hedrich-Blessing; illustration courtesy* Better Homes & Gardens, © *Meredith Corporation, 1963.*) *Right:* Excellent floor plan points up direct access to every room from front entry. (*Illustration courtesy* Better Homes & Gardens, © *Meredith Corporation, 1963*)

basic floor plan, and see how well (or poorly) its circulation will work for your family. How can you tell when you look at a house?

Six Tests for Good Circulation

The main traffic routes are the main paths the people in your family will use every day. They are the key to judging any house plan. Here they are:

(1) *The main entrance,* the front door, should funnel people, mostly visitors, directly to the living room. An entrance foyer is highly recommended for receiving guests. A coat closet nearby is virtually essential. The main entrance should be quickly and easily accessible from the driveway and street in front. It should also be quickly accessible from the rooms inside, where you are likely to be when the doorbell rings, and especially from the kitchen. The kitchen-to-front-door route is one of the most frequently used paths. A foyer is also important as a buffer or transfer chamber to keep howling winds, snow, and rain from blowing

into the heart of a house every time someone comes in the front door.

(2) *A separate family entrance,* ordinarily a back or side door, should lead directly into the kitchen area. This is the door most used by a family itself, especially the children. A proper location is important to permit swift unloading of groceries, for example. It should also be located so that children can travel in and out easily and can quickly get to where they're going inside the house (such as a nearby bathroom). The route from the car to this entrance should be sheltered from rain and from snow and ice in a cold climate. But the route from it through the kitchen should not run smack through the working area where a woman may be busy cooking.

(3) *The living room* should have a dead-end location for the reasons noted earlier plus a few others. It should not be a main route for everybody's travel around the house. Only then can you entertain guests in peace or just read or watch television without being continually disturbed by others walking through. Sometimes one end wall of the living room serves as a traffic lane; in effect, it's a hallway. That's all right if it happens to work in a particular house. Sometimes, though, a screen or half-wall may be necessary between it and the heart of the living room.

(4) *The room arrangement* should be designed so that you can go from any room in the house to any other without going through a third room except possibly the dining room. Direct access to a bathroom from any room is particularly important. Yet in some houses this rule is violated to the consternation of its occupants, and there are even houses in which access to a bedroom is possible only through a bathroom! If the bathroom is occupied, a person is trapped in the bedroom like a prisoner, unable to get out (unless he doesn't mind going out a window).

(5) *The kitchen* should have a central location. It should not be located way out in a left-field corner of the house. In the kitchen a woman should be close to the front door, should be able to over-see children playing in the family room, say, or outside, and should be able to get to the dining room, the living room, or the terrace without long hikes back and forth.

(6) *The main travel routes* between the house and the outdoor

Bad. This plan contains common flaws. For example, anyone coming in the front door gets a view of the living, dining, and kitchen areas.

Good. Rearranging the rooms in the same space sharply improves privacy for people inside, all out of view now of the front-door entry.

Bad. Garbled plan illustrates "Grand Central" living room, plus chopped-up house shape with every extra corner costing you money.

Good. Same number of rooms are rearranged logically, giving a private entrance, a zoned living room, much better circulation, and fewer corners to the house.

living areas—patio, terrace, or porch—should be short and direct. Can guests as well as family members go in and out easily? Is the outdoor area that you use most during pleasant weather easily accessible from the house? If it is, it will be used often. If not, you'll find it neglected and your family involuntarily depriving itself of outdoor-living benefits.

Those are the characteristics of a good floor plan. They're not always easy to get, which is why there are so many garbled plans. In fact, making a really efficient floor plan is one of the toughest things to do in the design of a house. This is why a good architect is essential. The importance of some of the individual tests will, of course, vary from family to family, depending on your own living habits and the activities you consider most important.

Bad. The living-dining area is one big hallway into the house. There's no privacy and little space for furniture.

Good. Moving the front-door entry to the side of the house and changing an interior door sharply improve plan. Adding door to kitchen gives convenient family entrance. (*Illustrations courtesy* Better Homes & Gardens, © *Meredith Corporation, 1963*)

If you like to spend a lot of time outside the house, for example, you may place high importance on efficient access to the outdoors. If you entertain often, you will place importance on the design and location of the dining room and living room for entertaining. And so on. The way you live, therefore, should be taken sharply into account so that your house will simplify daily living activities and make life a lot more pleasant.

Interior Zoning

Interior zoning is concerned with the logical arrangement of the rooms inside the house. Ideally, every house should have three clear-cut zones to accommodate the three main kinds of activities: living, sleeping, and working. The living zone embraces the living, dining, and family rooms, in which you engage in most activities other than working and sleeping. The work zone embraces the kitchen, laundry, and perhaps a workshop, where obvious, if not unavoidable, work of one kind or another goes on. The sleeping zone embraces the bedrooms. Each zone should be separate from the other. The two-story house provides natural zoning between the bedrooms upstairs and the other rooms downstairs with natural benefits. On the other hand, a garbled split-level house can turn

Interior of a modest Connecticut house is large, bright, and airy as a result of excellent open planning and large windows. Designed by architect Curt Sykora, house is located in Old Saybrook, Connecticut. (*Bill Hedrich, Hedrich-Blessing; illustration courtesy* Better Homes & Gardens, © *Meredith Corporation, 1963*)

your life into a nightmare if, for example, the living or working zone is on more than one level with utter disregard for the way people live in a house.

Regardless of the kind of house, a buffer wall or other such separation is essential between the bedrooms and the other two zones, if for no other reason than to permit you to entertain guests without disturbing children at study or in bed at night. The kitchen and work zone should be separate from the living area. Can dishes be left stacked and unwashed there without being seen by guests in the living room? Can laundry be left unfinished but out of view when visitors call unexpectedly (or even when they are expected)? The answer should be Yes. This type of question will tell you if a house plan has good zoning.

The Kitchen

The kitchen deserves top-priority attention. A woman usually spends more work time there than in any other single room. It also represents the highest-cost part of a house (because of its heavy-equipment concentration). Its cost will often run $20 to $30 per

Cheerful kitchen is made light and airy with large window facing south. Cabinets are made with a rugged Formica surface cover, which is very easy to keep clean. Designed by J. O. Watkins. (*All About Houses*)

Another view of same kitchen. Open shelves, on right, were a particular success. Not only are they less expensive than conventional cabinets, but they also give quick and convenient access to much-used dishes. (*All About Houses*)

square foot, or half as much again as the average square-foot cost of a typical house. The kitchen more than any other room also tends to influence the resale value of your house. It is clearly important, and its design elements should be reported in some detail.

A central location is the first requisite, as noted earlier. The kitchen also rates a good exposure in relation to the sun. The same principles apply as those given in the preceding chapter for overall orientation of a house. Best kitchen exposure is one with windows on the southeast; next best is south. That will let most bright light and sunshine flood in during the day for at least the eight months from September to April. It will mean a bright, airy kitchen most of the time when you want it, yet the same exposure is easy to shade on hot summer days.

A kitchen facing east gets sun in the morning, but that's about all. One facing west gets little or no sun except in the afternoon, and in summer it will get hit with particularly hot afternoon sun. A northern exposure is darkest and gloomiest of all, receiving the least sun and light the year around. The same exposure principles also apply to a dining room or other area that is used for most meals.

Kitchen Work Triangle

The heart of a kitchen is its "work triangle," the arrangement of the refrigerator, sink, and range in relation to each other. The entire process of efficiently preparing and cooking foods hinges on a good work triangle. From the refrigerator to sink to range should form a triangle with a total perimeter of at least twelve to fifteen feet, but no more than twenty-two feet, according to research at Cornell University's renowned kitchen laboratory. The appliances should be in that order to conform with the natural sequence of cooking.

Plenty of countertop space around the triangle is also a must. The University of Illinois Small Homes Council recommends these minimum standards: at least four and a half feet of countertop length on the open-door side of the refrigerator between the refrigerator and the sink; three and a half to four feet of countertop length between the sink and range; and at least two feet of countertop on the other side of the range. That adds up to a minimum of at least ten feet of countertop length in all. An additional two feet of countertop is desirable, if not essential, at or near the range as a last-step serving center, where food is put on plates before being taken to the table. If either the refrigerator, the sink, or the range is separate from the other triangle centers—on a separate wall, for example—extra countertop space should be placed at its side, in addition to the minimum standards just given.

Make sure the refrigerator door opens the right way—toward the counter between the refrigerator and sink, so food can be conveniently unloaded where you will want it. The wrong-door refrigerator is a common flaw. A separate wall oven can go almost anywhere. Once it's loaded, it can usually be turned on without demanding attention until the bell rings. A location near the range is not essential, but because of its heat, it ordinarily should not be put flush next to the refrigerator.

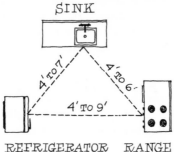

Kitchen work triangle shows minimum to maximum distances recommended for main work centers. (*All About Houses*)

An ample kitchen core and work triangle usually require a space at least eight by twelve feet (ninety-six square feet). That's the minimum to look for. With a dishwasher and separate oven, more space is needed. This should be an exclusive self-contained part of the kitchen out of the way of the main traffic routes used by people passing through the kitchen from one part of the house to another.

Kitchen Storage

According to studies at the University of Illinois, a minimum of at least eight and a half running feet of wall cabinets and/or storage shelves is recommended for the kitchen. Another rule calls for at least twenty square feet of interior storage space under the countertop plus at least ten square feet in wall cabinets. The proper cabinets and shelves should be located where they can house the particular items needed in each part of the kitchen—for example, storage for dishes and pots and pans near the sink and range; for working knives, bread box, flour, and other staples near the sink-refrigerator center; and so on.

Because kitchen cabinets can run into big money, consider open shelves for certain items. They can be a lot cheaper. If not enough cabinets or shelves are in a house, space should be available against walls or under the countertop to add what you'll need. The quality of cabinets is also important. You'll certainly want attractive cabinets with a rugged, hard finish that is easy to keep clean and will stay attractive over the years. The drawers should roll in and out easily, which calls for nylon rollers; try them and see. The cabinet hardware and latches should be of good quality.

Fixtures and Appliances

The best kitchen sinks are made of either stainless steel or enameled cast iron. Both are easy to keep clean and will retain their good looks over the years. There are also porcelain-on-steel sinks, which may look like cast iron; they are hard to keep clean, chip easily, and lose their gloss quickly. Sometimes the material of which it is made will be noted right on it; other times you must ask about it. You'll probably want a single-lever "one-armed" faucet rather than the old-style double-handle type. (More on faucets in Chapter 8.)

Appliances are largely a matter of personal preference. Sometimes when buying a house the appliances are optional, and you may bring along your own. You should know, however, which ones do or do not come, whether you are buying a new house or an old one. Those that are included should be noted in the sales contract to avoid a common misunderstanding that occurs when people buy houses. The buyer assumes he gets appliances but moves in and finds none. Clear this up before buying.

Final Checks for the Kitchen

Stand back and view the overall kitchen. It should be large enough to hold the table size required by your family, or an adequate dining area should be nearby. Some women also like space for a work desk and perhaps a sewing table. The laundry also should be nearby, or you may desire space in one part of the kitchen for a washer, dryer, and ironing board.

Are there electric outlets spaced behind the countertop for convenient use of small applicances? If not, how will you operate a mixer, a blender, and an electric frying pan as well as a toaster and a coffee maker? You'll want good lighting from above and lights that shed illumination over the full length of the countertop.

Here's how good design, including plenty of glass, can make a relatively small working kitchen bright, cheerful, and handsome. It's in a Pasadena, California, house designed by architect Neill Nobel. (*George de Gennaro; illustration courtesy* Better Homes & Gardens, © *Meredith Corporation, 1966*)

Finally, there's the need for good ventilation to keep the kitchen (as well as the rest of the house) free of cooking fumes and odors. A built-in exhaust fan is the least required. It should be located in the wall directly behind and above the range or in the ceiling directly over it. If located elsewhere, its exhaust efficiency will be low. A large range hood with built-in fan is even better. It should exhaust through a duct to outdoors. There are also "ventless" hoods equipped only with filters, with the hot air drawn through the filter and then spilled back into the kitchen; they do not cool a kitchen. Turn on the fan to check for noisy operation, a cause of widespread complaints. In a new house insist on a quiet one.

Bathroom Design

The location of the bathroom(s) is of first importance. There should be one located near the bedrooms. If it's the only one in the house, it should be convenient to other rooms as well.

Two or three bathrooms are usually essential for a large family, especially in a large or multilevel house. If an extra bathroom is wanted in a new house, order it when the house is being built, rather than after you move in. It can be installed for much less cost at that time than when the house is completed.

A big selling feature in new houses is the private bathroom for the master bedroom, but this is not always good design. In a two-bathroom house it might be better to locate the grown-ups' bathroom outside the master bedroom, where it is accessible to guests. Otherwise guests may be restricted to using the children's bathroom, which is often an embarrassing mess. Free the master bathroom, and the second bath can be given over completely to the children with no worry about the inevitable disorder found in it. This is unnecessary, of course, if a third bath or "powder room" is available for friends and visitors.

A full bathroom may be as small as five by seven feet and a half-bath (powder room) as small as twenty-four by forty inches or so. However, the key to adequate bathroom size is not the dimensions necessarily, but the number of people who are likely to be using it, particularly during the hectic morning rush hour. The more baths, the smaller the load on each and the less the need for large baths. You can usually tell by sight if a bathroom is large enough to handle two or three children or two grown-ups at once.

But extra bathrooms are not always necessary. A double lavatory, for example, may save you the expense of an extra bathroom. Two of them side by side can provide double-duty service from one bathroom. Sometimes a bathroom can be equipped with two toilet compartments, which also may be adequate and less costly than an extra bath. These are especially good ideas for families with children.

The quality of the fixtures in the bathroom is also important, and this is taken up in Chapter 8.

Other Rooms

A room should look and "feel" bright, cheerful, and pleasant. The presence of properly designed windows can make a huge difference. There should be enough unbroken wall area for easy furniture placement. Rooms should be large enough to accept your

Left: Bathroom built into a large space has luxuriously large tile counter and large mirror cabinet. Everything is first-rate except the low-quality faucets, the giveaway being the spoke handles. (*Tile Council of America.*) *Right*: Small bathroom has efficient lavatory with built-in hamper and large mirror cabinet. Note round hand-grip faucet handles, an indication of good quality. (*All About Houses*)

furniture. Good heating, adequate wiring, and lighting are also points to check. As for size and location, here are some minimum standards from the University of Illinois Small Homes Council. (Don't be put off by the word "small" in their name.)

• A living room at least twelve by twenty feet, with at least ten to twelve feet of unbroken wall for a couch. Remember, the living room should not be a major highway for traffic through the house, and the front door of the house should not open directly into it.

• A family room of at least twelve by sixteen, though twelve by

Large handsome glass doors give people dining in this room a beautiful private view outdoors. It also makes the room pleasant and large. (*Hedrich-Blessing for Andersen Corporation*)

twenty is better. It should be on the same level as the kitchen and near, if not adjacent to, the kitchen.

• Bedrooms at least nine by eleven and a half feet, with at least four square feet of closet space per person. The bedrooms should have privacy from the rest of the house, and the master bedroom in particular should have built-in privacy from the children's bedrooms. You'll notice, in fact, that almost every notable custom house published in architectural magazines will have the master bedroom located apart from other bedrooms, if not by itself on the other side of the house from children's rooms. Though it's not always easy to do in a low-priced house, it can be an excellent design feature in nearly every house.

Twenty-two Common Little Traps

The little things also count in a house. Here is a list of common design flaws found in houses. They include a few already noted in this chapter, which are repeated because of their importance.

• No separate entranceway or foyer to receive visitors.

• No opening in the front door, or no window or glass outlook alongside that lets you see who's at the door.

• No roof overhang or similar protection over the front door for shelter from rainy weather.

• No direct access route from the driveway to the kitchen.

• No direct route from outdoors to bathroom so children can come in and out with minimum of bother and mud-tracking.

• Gas, electric, and water meters inside the house or in the garage or basement, rather than outside. Outside meters do away with the need to let meter men in every month.

• Fishbowl picture window in the front of the house, exposing you to every passerby.

• The nightmare driveway that opens out on a blind curve so you cannot see oncoming traffic when backing out. A driveway that slopes up to the street is almost as bad, especially for trapping you hopelessly on a winter morning when your car won't start.

• Isolated garage or carport with no direct or protected access from car to house.

• Accident-inviting doors that open toward the basement stairs.

• Cut-up rooms with windows haphazardly located. Sometimes too many doors make it impossible to arrange furniture.

• Windows in children's rooms that are too low for safety, too high to see out of, and/or too small or difficult to get out of in case of fire.

• A hard-to-open window, usually the double-hung type, over the kitchen sink. An easily cranked casement window is usually best here; a sliding window second best.

• A window over the bathroom tub. This generally causes cold drafts as well as rotted windowsills as a result of condensation.

• Stage-front bathrooms placed squarely in view of a space like the living room or smack in view at the top of the stairway. Ideally, one should be able to go from any bedroom to the bathroom without being seen from another part of the house.

• Only one bathroom, especially tough on you in a two-story or split-level house.

• No light switches at every room entrance and exit.

• No light or electrical outlet on a porch, patio, or terrace.

• No outside light to light up the front path to and from the house.

• Noisy light switches that go on and off like a pistol shot. Silently operating switches cost only a little more, and no new house can be called modern without them today.

• Child-trap closets that can't be opened from inside.

• Small economy-size closets that are hardly big enough for half your wardrobe. Also watch out for narrow closet doors that keep half of the closet out of reach without a fishing pole, basketball-player shelves too high for a person of normal height, and clothes poles so low that dresses and trousers cannot hang without hitting the floor.

It should be clear by now that good design involves more than merely good looks (often deceptive) and surface glamour. The difference between a good design and the garbled-plan trap has to do with how well the house will *work* for you and your family.

The famous architect Le Corbusier aptly said that a house should be a "machine for living." His words stirred immediate anger in some circles where people reacted violently to the impersonal inference. But nonetheless it's an excellent phrase to remember when you inspect a house. Will the house serve you efficiently and well? Is it designed to permit you to carry out your everyday activities with ease and convenience in addition to providing pleasant and cheerful surroundings? Or is it a garbled plan that makes everyday activities a continual chore and burden?

If the plan is truly efficient, logically and sensibly designed for humans, it will come far closer to being a genuinely personal house. It will provide much satisfaction and continual pleasure every day you are in it. It will not be a garbled-plan trap.

The Old-House
Lemon

The experience of a young couple illustrates a common (and sad) mishap with old houses. By old houses, we mean any used house one year old or older. The couple bought a large old three-story house in downstate Illinois. It was on a pleasant street and was priced at a mere $19,500. It was rather run-down, they knew, but they were both young and eager to go to work on the house. It was a challenge. Besides, where else could they find such a big house at such a low price?

Taking stock of things two years later, they found they had poured over $8,000 into the house, plus much of their own labor over many nights and weekends. Yet there were still improvements to be made. It was a particularly cold winter, and it was then that the old furnace chose to stop working, which called for another $1,000 or so for a replacement.

That was too much. They decided to throw in the towel and sell it for $27,500, get their money back, and find another house.

Before. This old house, built in Piermont, New York, in 1840, went begging for a buyer. Like other relics, it represented a good buy only at the right price and only to people with the talent, willingness, and money to restore it to its original splendor. Priced for sale at $16,000 in the late 1950's, and probably not worth it, the owner finally sold it for $8,200. (*Don Blauhut*)

After. The same house restored and modernized—now the Blauhut house in Piermont—is a handsome and spacious example of nineteenth-century Federal architecture. (*Don Blauhut*)

This older house, built in the 1920's, is obviously in good, if not excellent, condition. Notice the new roof as well as the well-kept-up exterior wall siding. It's of no particular architectural style, and its design could be flawed by a purist, but it nonetheless can be a good value. (*All About Houses*)

Then came the final blow. The most they could get for the house was $22,500, which meant a $5,000 loss they could ill afford. They had been trapped by an old-house lemon.

They had made two mistakes. They had underestimated the amount of repairs and improvements that were needed, and they had overimproved the house for its location. As a result, they found that the value of the house did not grow, dollar for dollar, with the money they had poured into it.

There are three kinds of old houses. The first, the kind we would all like, is the old house—again any age—that is in good or excellent condition. The second is the kind that looks deceptively sturdy and solid but contains serious flaws that are often difficult to detect. This group includes houses that were built recently. It's hard to believe that anything could go wrong with them in such a short time, but their budding troubles usually started as a result of bad initial construction, or the house was put up by a vanishing builder, and the defects, like a progressive disease, take a little time to develop serious symptoms. Sometimes the first owner discovers his mistake and decides to get out from under and unload the place on another unsuspecting buyer.

The third kind of old house is the relic. Its run-down condition is far more obvious, however proud a house it was in the past. The perplexing thing is that people continually buy such houses with the delusion that they've discovered a rare bargain. Such a buyer knows that the house requires inevitable repairs and improvements. "But once fixed up," he says to his wife (or vice versa), "it will be a splendid house. Besides, it's loaded with 'charm.' " A psychological compulsion apparently drives certain people into buying the old relic. It's a human frailty, incomprehensible at times.

The moment of truth occurs when all those repairs and all that modernization not only are found to be inevitable but also add up to a whopping expense far beyond any initial estimates. Sometimes the old relic is so far gone that it is hopelessly irretrievable. The only realistic solution is to tear it down and build anew.

Why Buy an Old House?

There are nevertheless good reasons for buying *some* old houses. Many offer much more space than a new house at the same price, and all those rooms can hold irresistible appeal. An old house is often the only house available within convenient commuting distance of a job downtown in the city. The new houses being built are too far out in distant suburbs. Often an old house can be occupied immediately with little or no work required. There may be practically no moving-in expenses or costs for a new lawn, landscaping, or anything else of the kind associated with new houses. And with an old house you can generally move into an established neighborhood, with shade trees on the streets and little likelihood of new taxes like those often levied on new houses in expanding new suburbs.

It is also often remarked that old houses were built much better than new houses are, but this is frequently a myth. People will offer those old clichés, saying, "They don't build houses the way they used to," or, "You can't beat an old house for solid construction." To be sure, many splendid old houses boast thick old stone walls, handsome oak-plank flooring, and other nostalgic features like high ceilings, tile roofs, and hand-carved woodwork. They are lovely features of bygone age, seldom duplicated in new houses today.

The other side of the coin, however, is that new houses come with many a feature unknown in old houses: exciting modern kitchens and bathrooms, central heating and air conditioning, fuel-saving insulation, and rugged new materials and products which were formerly unknown but can now make a house exceedingly pleasant to live in. As far as the basic structure goes, a good new house today can be as strong, sturdy, and durable as the best old houses, if not more so.

An old house, however good, can also be difficult to buy because of the difficulty of financing it. A whopping down payment in cash is often required (unless, of course, you are lucky enough to obtain a low down-payment FHA or VA home loan). But by far the biggest pitfall to avoid is the old-house lemon, the kind that is riddled with shortcomings (to put it mildly) and in many cases is suffering from senility.

Obsolescence rates special mention. The older the house, the more likely vital parts will be worn and run-down. The usual furnace will last fifteen to twenty years, more or less, and repairs if not total replacement are inevitable. The usual roof covering is good for about the same period of time, after which it begins to crack and dry out, leaks start up, and a new roof cover must be bought. The wiring circuits become worn and frayed over the years and grow increasingly inadequate to handle all the new appliances and other electrical equipment that we pile into our homes. These and a variety of other items inevitably fall prey to wear and tear over the years, with the house naturally depreciating in value and function (though some owners refuse to admit it).

Every house requires upkeep, maintenance, and periodic modernization, but not every one gets it. On this score there's a special kind of old house to watch for warily. It's the one that has been in a family for years, though the children have long since grown up and left. The one or two surviving older people who stayed with the house do not mind a kitchen that is increasingly outmoded. There's only one operating bathroom, but that, too, is perfectly adequate for the small demands put on it. That kind of house for sale should flash a red danger flag before your eyes.

If you move in with a large family, it will soon become apparent that the house is incapable of meeting the heavy new demands put on it. Though formerly adequate for one or two older people, the plumbing will groan and begin to slow down because of the new strain put on it by a large active family. The furnace or the water heater or both, also asked to meet heavier demands for heating and hot water, will be forced to put out more, but neither can heat very well anymore. Similarly, the wiring and other parts of the house, which formerly could keep going under mild operating conditions, are not capable of coping with a hardy new group of occupants putting hardy new demands on the house. A variety of ailments sprout up.

How to Avoid the Old-House Lemon

How can you distinguish between the old house—again, a used house of any age—that's in fundamentally good condition and one that is not? There is only one surefire test. Have the house inspected by an expert, as Jack Briggs did and as logic and common sense demand. The cost will ordinarily run from about $50 to perhaps $100. That's the average range if you use one of the home-inspection services that have sprung up in recent years.

If you live in the New York metropolitan area, for example, try consulting engineer Arthur Tauscher (212 947-8184), one of the pioneers in the business. He started a firm called Home Inspection Consultants, Inc., with offices, so far, in Hackensack and Livingston, New Jersey; Philadelphia, Pennsylvania; Hartford, Connecticut; St. Louis, Missouri; and Denver, Colorado. For this or other such firms look in the classified telephone directory under "Home Inspection Services" or "Building Inspection Firms."

If you have trouble finding a qualified engineering expert, call the nearest FHA or VA office and ask the chief architect to recommend one. Ask whom his office uses, at least for termite and septic-tank checks, which are usually mandatory for houses submitted for government-insured mortgages. You could also try for a local builder or architect who is properly recommended, or search out a real-estate appraiser who, in addition to appraising the market value of houses, is technically qualified to inspect the structure and mechanical equipment in houses. Remember, though, that most appraisers are not conversant with the intricacies of house construction. If you talk with one, you should specify that you want a full structural check, not just the usual real-estate appraisal for market value only.

Using an expert is also recommended even when you buy a new house. He can judge the quality of construction for you and also spot inadvertent mistakes and construction oversights that you would overlook. With his report in hand you can request the builder to make the necessary corrections. He will usually be happy to do so before you buy the house (since he wants to make the sale) but perhaps not so willing after you buy.

How Much Will the House Really Cost?

Next step, determine the cost of essential repairs and modernization. If it is truly a fine old house, this cost should be small, but most houses require some work of one kind or another. Any way you look at it, a $30,000 house that requires $5,000 worth of work is a $35,000 house. It's as simple as that.

An old house in run-down condition can still be a bargain if its price plus the cost of essential work adds up to a reasonable figure. Of course, your total estimated investment in the house should be reflected in increased value. You don't want to overimprove too much. Some overimprovement can make sense if you intend to remain in the place for many years.

The Most Common Old-House Ailments

Following is a listing of the most common defects found in used homes, together with the approximate cost of repairing each. This can help you estimate the cost of fixing up an old house. Some of the common defects listed are found in young houses, too, including some of the most recently built used houses for sale.

The list adds up to nearly a dozen widespread flaws encountered in existing houses, but don't be alarmed by the number. You may encounter no more than two or three in a typical used house (excluding the old relic). The older the house, the more likely there will be numerous ailments. The cost figures are by necessity approximations and in some cases broad approximations. They are based on home-improvement prices in the early 1970's. Exact figures cannot be given, because labor rates vary so much from place to place, and costs also will vary greatly according to the complexity of a particular job and the amount of work required for a particular house. To get an accurate estimate for fixing up a house you must call in a contractor.

(1) and (2) *Old-fashioned kitchens and run-down bathrooms.* These are the two most prevalent shortcomings in old houses. You can judge the condition of each simply by looking. How much modernization will be required will depend on your personal standards. The kitchen in a house may satisfy you or may not. Don't kid yourself, though. Make a realistic appraisal of these key rooms. Full modernization of an obsolete old kitchen will ordinarily cost $2,500 to $5,000, possibly more if you want the very latest new kitchen and everything that that signifies.

A new half-bath installed where there was none before will usually cost about $750 to $1,500. Updating an obsolete full bathroom will generally cost at least $1,500 to $2,500.

(3) *Run-down heating.* If the house is hard to heat, fuel bills run astronomically high. Even then you still suffer chilly discomfort. The lack of proper insulation also enters the picture here. Because this problem is so common and ranks as a major trap, it is dealt with in detail in Chapter 9.

(4) *Defective septic-tank system.* If the house plumbing does not empty into a city sewer line, it usually empties into a septic-tank system or a cesspool. Be alerted, for septic-tank problems have reached virtually epidemic proportions in various parts of the country, especially in many recently built housing developments. Essential repairs or replacement can cost anywhere from $500 to $2,500. Determining the operating condition of the system is not always easy. If a house has a septic tank, ask the owner how well it works. Sometimes he'll say it's fine, though it isn't. Other times he'll frankly say that it isn't as good as it should be, but you can live with it until new city sewers are installed. Hooking up to a

sewer will cost at least a few hundred dollars. You can also call the local public health office and ask them how well septic tanks work in the area. Have serious troubles been experienced? Ordinarily they will know because of the health hazard involved.

The condition of a house cesspool may also be hard to determine. Some of them work for years without trouble; others don't. Like septic tanks, how well a cesspool works depends largely on the kind of soil. A porous soil that drains well is a good sign, since it readily absorbs sewage overflow. A hard, claylike soil is a bad sign. You can get further indication of possible trouble by determining—again from a good source like the health-department people—the kind of soil-drainage characteristics in the area and whether or not cesspools work well there.

(5) *Wet basement.* The basic problem stems from a chronic wet-soil condition coupled with poor drainage around a house. So much water piles up in the ground around a house that there is nowhere for it to go except to press through the foundation walls into the basement. Ordinary black asphalt waterproofing plastered on the walls won't necessarily keep it out either.

The problem is encountered most with a house located in low-lying ground, in a valley, or in an area surrounded by higher ground or hills from which rainwater flows down through underground streams. Conversely, a house set on a bluff or high ground is more likely to stay dry. So look around at the terrain for the telltale high-ground sources of shed water that can endanger the basement. Ask the owner if the basement stays dry after a heavy rain (he may or may not give you an honest answer). How he answers can be revealing. Check the basement yourself for signs of water stains, particularly on the walls facing the high ground outside. A chronic wet basement should be avoided, because it can cause wood-rot problems and spread mildew throughout the house.

Sometimes, however, the problem is easily licked simply by improving the soil drainage around the house, which will cost very little. Sometimes you can do it yourself with a shovel. Often it's caused by defective downspout runoff of water from the roof, and this, too, is relatively easy and inexpensive to correct. If the problem is chronic, however, the remedy can cost as much as $1,000 or more. The ground must be dug up all around the foundation walls, the walls must be properly waterproofed, and, in addition, a new drain-tile system must be installed in the ground outside the foundation footings (the base of the house).

(6) *Puny wiring.* The older the house, the more likely the wiring is obsolete and inadequate. This is because of the skyrocketing electrical demands in houses as a result of the hordes of new appliances that have been introduced. In 1940, for example, only a dozen or so different kinds of electrical items were used in the home. A mere 30-ampere electric service was all you needed to power a house, including the lights. Now there are close to a *hundred* different electric devices of one kind or another found in the home—everything from washers and dryers to electric toothbrushes, TV sets, and electric knife sharpeners. Some of them, such as an electric dryer or a range, draw more electricity than could be supplied by the entire electric board in a 1940 house.

The average house today requires an electric service input of 240 volts and 100 amperes capacity. It should say at least that— 240 volts, 100 amperes—on the main electric switchbox. That's where the fuses or circuit breakers are located. If it's a large house or if it has heavy electric users like electric heat or air conditioning or say, an electric range or a dryer, you should look for at least 240 volts and 150 to 200 amperes capacity.

Inspect the main electric board. If it's a small one with a rating of less than 100 amperes, a new electric service is likely to be needed. The cost will run from about $150 to $300. You are also likely to need rewiring, if not new wiring circuits, new switches, and new outlets in various parts of the house. Figure from $8 to $11 apiece for each new switch and double outlet you'll need plus $25 to $60 roughly for each new heavy-appliance outlet needed for equipment like an electric dryer. In all, the total cost of new wiring for a typical seven- or eight-room house will run from about $350 to $750, and more for a larger house.

(7) *Clogged-up plumbing.* Clogged-up plumbing is most likely in houses built prior to World War II, since corrosion-resistant copper and bronze plumbing was not introduced for housing until just before World War II. Before then, iron and steel pipes were the rule. Over several decades such piping tends to choke up with rust and corrosion, like cholesterol chokes off the blood flow in human arteries. In time, little or no water can get through, and the

plumbing must be replaced. Some younger houses in certain areas will also have iron or steel plumbing pipes, which is not a good sign. Nonferrous copper or bronze pipes last much longer.

A small magnet can let you know the kind of piping in a house, assuming it is not evident to the eye. Hold the magnet near the pipes. It will be drawn to iron or steel but not to copper or bronze.

If the plumbing consists of an old set of iron or steel pipes, chances are it is going downhill, particularly if the water only trickles out of the faucets. Turn all the faucets on at once in a bathroom (an upstairs bathroom in a multifloor house). Make it a real test by flushing the toilet at the same time. If the water slows to a trickle, it's not good. It could well signify serious trouble. New plumbing can cost from $1,000 to $2,500, and more for large houses.

Sometimes, however, low water pressure is caused by insufficient water pressures from the street. Actually, this problem is usually caused by too small a water-supply line to the house from the street. A new and larger line is the remedy at a cost ranging from about $350 to perhaps thrice that, depending on the digging distance from the house to the street waterline.

(8) *Termite and wood-rot damage.* First, there's no need to panic if there are termites. They may have entered relatively recently, and it usually takes a few years before they get a foothold in a house and cause real damage. If, however, they've been having a ball inside the house for some time, things can be quite serious. You may not discover the party going on until the piano falls through a weakened floor.

Termites have now spread to virtually every state in the nation except Alaska. They can burrow into the substructure of a house through cracks and holes a mere $\frac{1}{32}$ inch in diameter. They usually come up from the ground below the house, which means coming up into cement-floor houses (no basements) with virtually no visual signs of their arrival. You can't see them unless you happen on one of their camouflaged little mud tunnels and break it open, or cut into a beam they've infiltrated. An expert, however, knows where to look for them. A minor termite condition can sometimes be corrected for a few hundred dollars, but a major one can require several thousand dollars' worth of repairs.

Wood rot is often mistaken for termite damage because of the

To the casual home-buyer termites might look like dirt streaks. Sometimes they travel up through cracks inside the walls, with virtually no visible evidence of their presence. (*All About Houses*)

simliarity of appearance. It is caused by a fungus that attacks wood, eating and dismembering it much like termites. It causes even more widespread damage than termites and can call for much timber replacement in a house. The man you hire for a termite check should also give you a report on the extent, if any, of wood rot.

(9) *Sagging structure*. Major shoring up is a distinct possibility. Every house will settle a little over the years. But if the structure is wrenched severely out of shape, something drastic is wrong. Stand back a few feet from each corner of the house, and sight down each of the four walls. The lines should be square and true. A major bulge or awkward protuberance can spell trouble. A few inches out of plumb can be expected and is usually of no importance. Notice if the windows and doors line up squarely with each other and with the house frame. Windows and doors should open and close easily—that is, no binding.

What you see can indicate whether or not a house is in serious trouble. A contractor can estimate the cost of repairs. Some new

This is the worker termite, about a half-inch long actual size, distinguished by a large head, grayish-white color, no wings, and no narrowing at the waist. It's rarely seen unless you break into one of its tunnels. The swarming termite seen in spring has a black body, glassy wings, and also no narrowing at the waist. The flying ant, on the other hand, does have a narrow waist, which is one way to tell it from a termite. (*All About Houses*)

supporting posts in the cellar may be all that's needed at relatively low cost. Major work on the underpinnings can cost several thousand dollars.

(10) *Worn-out roof and rain gutters.* The condition of the roof can usually be judged simply by looking for broken, cracked, or missing shingles. Take a close look at the flashing around the chimney. That's where the first leaks generally show up. A typical asphalt-shingle roof, the most common cover on houses, will ordinarily last fifteen to twenty years before reroofing is required. It may wear out faster in the hot South, where the overhead sun is murderous, and last longer in northern states. A roof more than fifteen to twenty years old is likely to be a trouble spot.

New roofing for an old house will generally cost between $20 and $35 a "square" (one hundred square feet of roof area). The exact price depends on local labor rates, the material used, and complications caused by roof jogs and breaks. The total cost of a new roof for the average house will, at those rates, run about $500 to $1,000. Gutters can be troublesome, too, especially if they are filled with leaves or are worn out and broken. Figure another $150 to $350 if the gutters need replacement or repairs.

(11) *Worn-out water heater.* Replacing this little essential tank is a comparatively small expense ($150 to $200), but it's a

common one. Many water heaters are undersized, so you run out of hot water in the middle of a shower, bath, or clothes wash. A good many low-grade water heaters are found in houses. They sometimes last no more than three to four years, then spring a leak and must be replaced.

Check the water heater for adequate capacity. Most families require a forty-to-fifty-gallon tank, though thirty gallons may be large enough if the nameplate says it is a "rapid recovery" model. Those are *minimum* capacities for gas and oil models. Electric water heaters should range from eighty gallons capacity and up. A smaller sixty-gallon size will do only if the nameplate says it's a "high speed" or "high watt" model or if your family is small and has modest hot-water needs.

Also check the condition of the heater. The first signs of impending failure are rust and cracks at the bottom of the tank and sometimes a small leak, with water running onto the floor. You can check these things by looking at the bottom of the unit with a flashlight.

The Final Judgment

A few final words about buying an old house. It's a good idea to spend an hour or two going over the house, even though you have hired an expert for a professional inspection. This is not to say that you should be your own expert. A personal inspection, however, can give you a good insight into the house.

Besides the common flaws just listed, notice the condition of the house inside and out. Are the floors and woodwork in good shape? How do the attic and basement shape up? What about the workmanship? Look at the floor around the bathroom tub and shower and at the kitchen floor below the sink and at the base of the cabinets. These are chronic splash-water areas, where evidence of rot and deterioration often shows up first. Observe the condition of the foundation walls. Does the masonry contain many cracks and holes? (A few are inevitable in nearly every house.) In short, give the place a good, if not expert, going-over.

How do you feel now about the condition of the house? Right here you will begin to get a distinct impression of the house. If you have nagging doubts about it, don't push them out of your mind simply because you want to like the house. When you get home, sit down, and let your true feelings rise to the surface. A husband and wife can exchange views. Is it really a good house, or does it spell trouble? It may have a few flaws, but practically every house does. Is it really worth the price asked? Or is it worth buying only if you get it at a reduced price (to allow for repairs)?

Ask yourself questions like these as you reflect about the house, and then answer them realistically. Sure, some houses are not all you may like, but if your standards are set too high, you may never find one that will suit. On the other hand, what your deep-down feelings honestly are about the house, whether it is really a good one for you or not, can be the best indication of whether or not to buy it.

The key to this judgment is facing up to your basic feelings about the house and recognizing them for what they are. If you realize that the house stirs serious doubts in you, watch out; but if the house has been checked by an expert, if it has no serious flaws, and if you really like it and want it, then you've found a good house.

The Marginal House

The marginal house is the one that just squeaks by. The quality of its construction and the parts that went into it is marginal. It's not necessarily a substandard house. The house very likely comes up to the local building code and sometimes even FHA's minimum standards, but nevertheless it's a marginal house.

This is no news to the knowledgeable homeowner who has bought one or more houses, particularly if one was a low-quality cracker box. It could also have been a supposedly good house of higher-than-average cost. One such couple knows well the trouble, irritation, and extra expense a marginal house represents. There was the summer vacation that went down the drain because money was needed for a new paint job, though at the time the house was a mere three years old. There were the children's chilly bedrooms which were impossible to heat during cold weather, in spite of the high fuel bills. There were the paper-thin walls and the cheap paneling that looked deceptively handsome when they first moved in but soon began to wear thin and tawdry like cheap wallpaper. And there was also the low-grade flooring, especially in the kitchen and bathroom, which was impossible to keep clean and good-looking.

Why So Much Marginal Quality?

There is so much marginal quality because nearly everything that goes into a house—the flooring, wall products, roofing, siding, heating, wiring, paint, and virtually every other product—can be had in more than one grade or in some cases more than one weight or thickness. Naturally, the lowest grade costs the least in initial price, just as the lowest-grade beef and eggs and the cheapest quality of clothing material carry the lowest price tags. The lowest-grade economy materials are used widely in house construction to keep down costs. They are designed to meet certain *minimum* standards. What's more, marginal quality is not limited to low-priced houses. It's also prevalent to a degree in many high-priced houses, which means houses priced at $50,000 or more.

The lowest-grade marginal products actually cost you money in the long run and often in the short run, too. In time their performance trails off. They require more and more upkeep and maintenance and time and expense. They usually have a shorter life than the high-quality grades of the same products. That can call for early replacements, again with the homeowner paying extra. All these things add up to a marginal house that becomes a growing source of nagging annoyance and bother.

Moreover, really good if not top-notch quality building products often cost only a little more than the lowest-grade ones. You don't have to pay Cadillac prices for top construction quality. The very best quality house paint, for example, costs only a dollar or two more per gallon than the minimal grade usually used on houses. Using that best paint on a typical $35,000 house will increase the total paint cost by a mere $20 to $25. The cost of the labor to apply the paint does not increase. Yet you get a far more durable exterior paint job that will last up to twice as long as marginal paint, which means, among other things, reduced repainting expenses.

High-quality flooring, paneling, wiring, heating, and many other products similarly cost only a little more, by and large, than the same products in marginal quality. Like top-notch paint, each is more durable, lasts longer, and requires less upkeep, cleaning, and maintenance than its marginal-quality counterpart, and the cost of installing high-quality materials is generally no greater than the cost of installing marginal materials. Virtually the same amount of labor is required to put down a new floor, for example, regardless of whether the best- or worst-quality flooring is used. The principle of quality also applies to such things as the masonry work, like the foundation of a house. High-quality masonry simply requires the use of a few extra bags of cement in the mix, raising the construction cost of a typical house by about $40 to $50, and that's all.

The Cost of Quality

Studies show that the initial price of a house built with high-quality materials will run only about 8 to 10 percent more than the price of an identical house built of marginal-quality materials. But that extra amount takes only a small bite out of your pocketbook because of the way the financing works. In fact, you will actually save money.

Say, for example, that you plan to buy a typical new house for $40,000, and more often than not it is likely to be a marginal house. It may be a serviceable house, meeting all the codes (which are minimum standards). It will be no better and no worse than many other new houses. Assume further that you can buy the house with 25 percent down, $10,000 cash, and a $30,000 mortgage which calls for payments on principal and interest of $222 a month.

Now say that you request the builder to give you the same house built according to high-quality standards—a top-notch heating plant, more insulation, really good bathroom fixtures, the best paint, and other high-quality construction features. The house price should go up to about $44,000, or 10 percent more. A 25-percent down payment would now come to $11,000, or $1,000 more than before. The mortgage goes up to $33,000. At the same

High-quality flooring is essential for attractive long-lasting floors. This is quarry tile, an excellent material for the heavily trafficked entrance of a house. A few handsome, high-quality features and products like this, which are obvious at first glance, generally indicate a high-quality house, as opposed to a questionable or marginal house. (*All About Houses*)

interest rate as before, this calls for payments of $244 a month, or $22 more than for the marginal house.

But you will get that extra cost back plus a dividend each month after you move in. The studies show that the high-quality house will save you, on the average, about $450 to $600 a year, or $15 to $28 a month saved over the years. These are your savings on upkeep, maintenance, and inevitable repairs as a result of high-quality construction materials. You will also save time and effort on all those little maintenance chores that crop up in houses as well as cut down on the amount of weekly housework (to keep floors and walls clean and attractive, for instance).

In sum, the high-quality house makes sense in every way. Conversely, the marginal house is a snare and a trap—a snare because it costs less at first and a trap because it ends up costing you more, sometimes considerably more (when major things wear out and must be replaced at high expense). Money aside, the high-quality house really pays for itself in the extra satisfaction and living benefits that you receive, as with virtually any other high-quality product you may buy.

How to Avoid the Marginal House and Get a Better Deal

How do you tell the difference between the marginal house and a really good house? It comes down to knowing the distinguishing traits of good-quality products and materials.

If you are buying a new house of marginal quality, as determined by inspection of the builder's model or his blueprints, you simply request that the house to be built for you contain better-quality materials. Give him a list of the changes you want. Most builders will accommodate you, though they will, of course, charge you for each change. If you think you are being overcharged, check the additional cost for the quality materials you want with the particular supplier involved—for example, a plumbing-supply house for bathroom-fixtures prices, a heating contractor for the cost of his best furnace, the lumberyard for building-materials prices, and so on.

You may also save money by having the builder omit certain features ordinarily included in the house which you consider of small importance. The model house may contain a fancy intercom system, say, or a finished downstairs recreation room, or other such features usually included more for their initial sales appeal than for function. If they appeal little to you, consider trading them off for extra quality in the house. Your extra cost for the house will come down.

If you are considering an already built new house that is of marginal quality, unfortunately there is little you can do about it. You can buy it as is, accepting its shortcomings, or pass it up. Sometimes, however, if you really like the house, a builder will build another one for you with the higher-quality standards you specifically request.

If you are considering a used house, obviously you can do little to change its construction quality. But by knowing about good-quality construction you can avoid the marginal house and aim for one that is well built.

What about FHA Quality?

How much extra construction quality do you get if you buy an FHA house? That, of course, is a house that has been approved for an FHA mortgage. Consider first a new house that was approved for FHA financing before construction on the house began (which also means that the house qualifies for FHA's four-year major-defects warranty, as noted in Chapter 4).

Buying a new FHA house is a big step in the right direction. It means the house is built according to FHA's Minimum Property Standards. (But note again that word "minimum"!) Many parts of the house will be of higher-than-average quality, but by no means all. By and large, FHA's construction rules, its building standards, are stiffer and more uncompromising than any other building standards in effect for houses today. But they do not mean that you will get uniformly high quality throughout the house. The FHA rulebook covers hundreds of things in a house. Sad to say, not all of them are high-quality specifications. Some are written so that minimum quality will easily get by. You therefore must go a step further to avoid marginal quality even in an FHA house.

Suppose you are buying a used house with an FHA mortgage. You could still get a marginal house, although there is less likelihood of getting a defective house. An FHA inspector will check the house. Comparatively speaking, the FHA (and VA) inspections are quite thorough, but because of the nature of used houses, not only is a comprehensive structural evaluation impossible, but the quality of construction need meet only minimum standards. It could be a house of marginal quality and still get FHA (or VA) approval.

By the way, a copy of FHA's construction standards can help you whether you're buying a new or an old house, with or without an FHA mortgage. This is a comprehensive construction guide with over three hundred pages called *Minimum Property Standards*, written by the Federal Housing Administration. It can be obtained for $2 from the Superintendent of Documents, Government Printing Office, Washington, D.C. 20402.

The Hallmarks of the Quality House

Here is a summary of high-quality features to look for when you buy a house.

(1) *Foundation walls* of poured concrete, also called cast-in-place walls, are usually better than concrete-block or cinder-block walls. Poured walls offer better natural waterproofing and are more durable and far more resistant to termites. The best quality requires a good cement mix. The use of one extra sack of cement per cubic yard, compared with the usual practices, can virtually ensure high-quality strength and permanence.

Concrete-block walls should be pargeted (plastered) with a half inch of cement mortar on the outside. Much extra strength is gained if they are also laced with joint reinforcement rods. These would be placed in the mortar beds between courses of block—generally every few courses.

Whichever type of foundation, ask for troweled-on waterproofing instead of the usual brush-on or spray-on type. If local water conditions are bad, protection can be further improved with a film of polyethylene or asphalt-impregnated membrane. Running this film right down to the base of the footing will seal all joints. Another good waterproofing material is bentonite clay panels, which are placed against the foundation before backfilling.

A system of tile drainpipe should be put in the ground around the house at the base of the foundation walls, except in dry areas. This gets rid of groundwater that would otherwise get into the basement. It is often the only way to keep the basement dry. Insist on it if you want to avoid a wet basement.

(2) *Termite protection* is recommended in nearly all states but Alaska. You can use either soil chemicals, chemically treated timber, or termite shields. As noted before, a poured-concrete foundation will provide additional protection.

(3) *Exterior walls* should be rugged and durable, with a long-lasting finish. Prefinished wall siding is highly recommended to reduce repainting. This includes prefinished hardboard or wood, aluminum siding, galvanized steel, plywood, mineral-fiber sidings. Such materials should have a name brand. The best kinds are guaranteed—the longer the guarantee, the better.

If the walls are painted, insist on top-of-the-line paint, the very best. It should be a well-known brand. Get a three-coat job—a primer and two finish coats. Make sure the siding is applied with double galvanized, aluminum, or other rustproof nails. Be sure each nailhead is set below the surface of the wood and covered with putty. Also be sure that any joints between siding boards are puttied over and that all window and door trim is properly caulked with one of the new rubber-based caulking compounds that stay flexible.

(4) *Interior walls* are usually made of ½-inch plasterboard today, which is basically satisfactory and better than the ⅜-inch plasterboard sometimes used. Even better is the ⅝-inch thickness. Best of all, particularly for superior sound control and a nail-free surface, is a two-layer wall in which one layer of ⅜-inch plasterboard is laminated over another. With either one- or two-layer walls, the builder should use three layers of compound over joints and nailheads.

On paneled walls prefinished materials give easier cleaning, plus resistance to soiling, marring, and stains. Wood paneling gains fire resistance if applied over plasterboard or asbestos-cement board instead of directly to the framing members. With plaster two coats over metal lath is good; three coats is better, though rarely done today.

(5) *Flooring* should be closely fitted and display no wide gaps and no high edges. That goes for hardwood strips or block as well as resilient flooring. No squeaks should be heard when you walk over it slowly. The appearance of hardwood flooring varies according to the wood used—oak and maple are the king and queen of the hardwoods—and also according to grade. For example, the highest-grade, finest-grained oak is "Clear," which costs two to three cents more a square foot than the second grade, "Select," which in turn runs about three to five cents more per

The little things count big. Drawers slide in and out on rollers, providing quick access to supplies. Shelves are designed for standard food packages. (*Illustration courtesy* Better Homes & Gardens, © *Meredith Corporation, 1966*)

square foot than "No. 1 Common." With wooden floors ask for a top-grade polyurethane floor finish, which will glisten for a year or so without waxing.

Resilient flooring starts with asphalt tile, the cheapest and lowest quality; it's good for a concrete basement floor, but that's about all. Next in price comes asphalt asbestos tile, a questionable material in a hard-wear location. Finally there are pure vinyl, rubber, and cork tiles. Pure vinyl is best for most uses. Rubber has only fair resistance to oil and grease. Cork can look exceedingly rich and handsome but will soon look worn in heavy-traffic rooms. There is also sheet linoleum, the granddaddy of composition flooring, which is cheap. It is easily hurt by water and is therefore not the best material for kitchens and bathrooms. Get the heaviest gauge available and definitely the "inlaid" kind; cut through a sample, and you should see that the grain goes all the way through from one surface to the other.

(6) *Windows and doors* should be a well-known national brand, such as Anderson, Malta, and Pella. They should fit tightly, open and close easily, and be easy to clean from inside. Weather stripping should be built into the frames; you should see it. Aluminum windows should contain plastic fittings which prevent a direct connection (thus no cold flow) between the movable parts and the frame. The best kind come with provisions for easily slipping in a screen and a storm-glass panel. In a cold climate double-glass windows (such as Thermopane or Twindow) can pay in better comfort, particularly in a new house, where they save the cost of storm windows. Double-glass windows will cost, all told, about 10 to 20 percent more than the combined cost of ordinary single-pane glass windows plus storm windows.

(7) *The kitchen countertop surfaces* should be a plastic laminate (Formica, Micarta, or Panelite) or possibly ceramic tile, which is even tougher, though it's hard on dropped chinaware. The best kitchen cabinets are those of a brand-name manufacturer with a rugged factory-applied finish. Steel cabinets should be heavy-gauge material (feel them in different houses).

There should be enough electric outlets behind the countertop for plugging in small appliances, and one or two double outlets where the kitchen table will go. Overhead lighting should flood the length of the countertop; one light in the middle of the room is not enough.

(8) *Each bathroom fixture* should show the imprint of a national manufacturer (Briggs, "Standard," Eljer, and Richmond are some). This is important because the same manufacturers do not stamp their name on their lowest-quality fixtures. An enameled cast-iron tub has the edge over the enameled-steel kind. Cast iron

A good shower head swivels to any direction, is self-cleaning, has adjustable spray control, and retains its gleaming appearance. (*Speakman Company*)

Handsome ceramic tile shower stall is easy to keep clean and provides long-lasting waterproof walls. Small buttonlike accessory on the faucet is diverter control for shower nozzle. (*All About Houses*)

is less apt to chip or wear and comes in more styles and sizes. Tall people who like to take tub baths should be sure the tub is long enough. They range in length from six feet long down to pygmy length. The depth inside will vary from 15¼ inches down to a shallow 12½ inches. You'll probably want the deepest kind, not only for baths, but also because it will mean less water splashing on the floor.

Flushing action is the key to toilet quality. Cheapest of all is a wash-down model, which is poorest and the least sanitary. Next steps up in quality are: the reverse-trap action unit; the siphon jet, which is quite good; and the siphon-jet vortex, best of all and the kind used for the luxury one-piece quiet-flush toilets. The one-piece wall-mounted toilet makes cleaning the bathroom easier, though it has a luxury price tag. Whatever the toilet model, test it for noise and effectiveness by flushing it.

The best lavatory bowls are made of gleaming vitreous china. They are only slightly more expensive than enameled cast iron, which is next best. There are also enameled steel bowls, third in quality and more susceptible to chipping and wear.

When you judge the lavatory basin, think big. It should be large enough for comfortable use, especially if you use it for washing your hair or for bathing an infant. There are skimpy sizes as small as 15 by 17 inches and large ones up to about 28 by 20 inches. Try for at least 20 by 24; these cost only about $5 or so more than the smallest ones.

Good faucets are made of solid brass with a tough coat of chrome, nickel, or brushed or polished brass. The marginal kind are usually made of lightweight zinc or aluminum castings, which tarnish quickly, drip, and look dreadful within a short time. The cheapest kind can often be identified by their crosslike handle, four horizontal spokes coming out from the center. The solid-brass kind generally has a solid handle with grooves for your fingers. There are also deluxe faucets, a third grade which offer little extra in quality. They cost considerably more for such luxury features as push-pull or dial control or for a monogrammed or Lucite handle. Single-lever-control faucets are also available and good; they offer ease of operation as well as good quality. This applies to the kitchen faucet as well as to those in bathrooms.

The shower nozzle should have a flexible ball point for direction control and a spray control. These nozzles are self-cleaning. The cheap kind generally offers little or no control of direction or spray quality. An "automatic diverter control" should come with a combination shower-tub. It automatically diverts the water back to the tub faucets after someone has showered and so prevents the next person, who may want to take a tub bath, from being pelted with hot or cold water when he turns on the faucets. Omission of the diverter, an inexpensive item, can also cause accidental scalding of children.

Bathroom accessories should include a large medicine cabinet, which means at least thirty inches wide and twenty inches high. The doors should open easily. Other features are built-in linen closets, laundry hampers, a separate medicine cabinet with lock and key for safekeeping of pills and medicines that could harm children (a good place for it is high in the linen closet out of reach of kids), and good lighting, preferably with incandescent bulbs, since the usual fluorescent bulbs give a cold, harsh light that makes people look ghoulish.

Waterproof floors and walls, particularly around the tub and shower, are also essential. Ceramic tile is the old proven wall and floor material, and you can hardly go wrong with it. It is not necessarily essential for the walls, except for the shower cubicle. There are also rugged new plastic wall materials, such as melamine-coated hardboard, which are very good. Not all are good, however, so if in doubt about the kind you see, check on its quality with a local tile-supplier.

As for the flooring, avoid linoleum and asphalt tile in the bathroom. They quickly fall prey to water rot, and they are hard to keep clean and attractive. The flooring should be a tough pure vinyl or comparable material—ceramic tile or, say, marble or terrazzo.

Also check the bathroom for safety features such as grab bars in the shower (to prevent falls); a waterproof shower light; electric outlets well out of reach of the shower, tub, and lavatory water (to prevent being electrocuted); and good-quality soap holders and towel racks. Be sure there are shutoff valves at each fixture (so the water can be turned off for repairs without turning off the main water supply to the house).

(9) *Good plumbing* starts even before the water meter. The water-supply pipe from the street to the meter should be at least ¾ to 1 inch in diameter, rather than the more usual ½ inch. That will ensure ample water pressure for the house. Copper pipe should be a must; it is now standard in many areas. Shutoff valves at every fixture are also a must. You should see them behind the kitchen sink as well as in the bathroom. An antiwater-hammer setup will cut down pipe pounding and also reduce faucet wear. Hot-water lines to distant bathrooms should either be insulated or have a hot-water recirculating line to provide instant hot water, particularly in winter.

(10) *The water heater* for gas or oil should ordinarily have a tank capacity of forty to fifty gallons and at least eighty gallons if electric, as noted in Chapter 7. In a new house the kind of guarantee given on it is the tip-off to quality. It should be guaranteed for at least ten years; anything less is marginal.

If the water heater is an integral part of the hot-water boiler used for heating the house, minimum rating for a one-bath house is 2.75 gpm (gallons per minute of hot water); at least 3.25 gpm for two baths, more for a large family and large house. The rating will be on the boiler, which also should have an IWH seal of good quality. That stands for an approved Indirect Water Heater. If there's no IWH seal, the quality is probably poor.

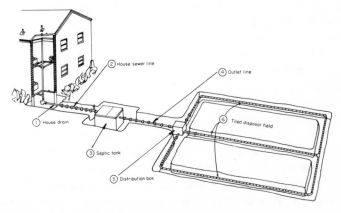

This shows how a septic-tank system for household sewer disposal is put underground. Find out the location of the septic tank when you buy a house so that it can be easily found for cleaning. (*All About Houses*)

Main electric board, center, has 240-volt capacity and twenty circuit breakers. (*All About Houses*)

(11) *A septic tank* should have a capacity of at least 900 gallons for a three-bedroom house, 1,000 gallons for a four-bedroom, at least 1,250 gallons for five or more bedrooms. It is best when the tank and its piping system (leaching field) are located in front of the house. That will facilitate the lowest-cost, most-direct connection to the sewer later.

A percolation test is the real measure of septic-tank quality. This tells you how well the soil will absorb septic wastes and thus the size of the septic-tank system required. A test hole of four to twelve inches in diameter is dug in the ground, two inches of gravel is placed at the bottom, and at least twelve inches of water is poured over the gravel. The water is left standing at least four hours and preferably overnight. The absorbing quality of the soil is determined by how long it takes for the water level to fall one inch. Properly carried out, the test will tell you whether or not a septic tank will work well and also how large a set of distribution pipes is required under the ground. The test should be carried out by an expert, preferably from the local health department. It is up to the home-buyer, however, to find out if it was done and what the results were. It is important because many health experts estimate that in as many as 50 percent of all houses septic-tank systems do not work right.

(12) *The electrical wiring* should be supplied by a 240-volt three-wire feed from the telephone pole—you can actually see three wires—to a 240-volt electric board in the house. The main board should have a capacity of at least 100 amperes, but that's the absolute minimum recommended today. Look for a rating of 150 to 200 amperes noted on the board if electric heat is used or if it is a big house and you have a lot of electrical equipment.

Inside the board there should be at least fifteen to twenty individual circuit breakers (preferred over fuses) rather than a skimpy eight or ten. There is one circuit breaker per wiring circuit. A board with extra circuits is very cheap if it is installed originally and much more expensive if you have to get one later.

Additional Features

The heavier asphalt roofing is, the longer it will last. Asphalt roof shingles of 235 pounds per "square" (one hundred square feet of shingling) in weight are the lightest you should accept. A superior grade is the "heavyweight" type which are asphalt shingles rated at 290 pounds per square, or better. They should be either the seal-down or the glue-tab kind to stay put on a roof in an area where violent windstorms or hurricanes occur.

Roof gutters and flashing of copper are traditionally noted for durability. Galvanized steel gutters are the usual kind and must be kept painted inside and out. They are better if they have a baked-on factory finish. Aluminum and vinyl gutters are better.

The door hardware should be solid brass, solid bronze, or solid aluminum. These materials are noted for long service; they also retain surface finish far longer than the usual iron or steel hardware that has a plated finish and may look solid but is not. Outside door locks should have a deadlock latch mechanism.

The attic should be fitted with large air-vent louvers, not the small kind. These not only help cool the house in summer but also provide essential attic ventilation the year around (to prevent condensation and wood-rot problems under the roof).

The Discomfort House

Some years ago a $160,000 consumer survey was made to determine what made the home-buyer tick. Why do home-buyers seek new houses? What are the biggest things wrong with their present houses that make people want new ones?

Among the people interviewed the number-one source of dissatisfaction was, not surprisingly, "too small a house." The biggest reason for buying a new house was to get more space. The next-largest cause of dissatisfaction was a surprise: bad heating. A large number of people apparently want to flee from discomfort houses.

From the same group of people, a sampling representing 30 million American families, the greatest number (63 percent) also said that the most important feature they desired in a new house was adequate heating. (The next most important features cited were: a house that won't be too much of a financial burden, 54 percent; enough electric power and wiring, 46 percent; good insulation, 33.2 percent; and low property taxes, 33 percent.)

A well-designed house can combine the exciting outdoor vista provided by large glass walls and still be warm and comfortable indoors in winter, cool and quiet in summer. Double-thickness, insulating glass reduces cold entry indoors, and combination heating-cooling outlets, located in the floor directly under the glass, put up an additional fence of warm or cool air for indoor temperature control. (*Carl Ullrich, Inc.*)

Other consumer surveys confirm the great concern shown about house heating. They also confirm what is clearly a widespread problem in houses: poor heating and the resulting chilly discomfort. In sum, they point up that the discomfort house is a major home-buying trap.

Heating by itself rates special mention for another reason. After mortgage payments and taxes it generally accounts for the biggest annual expense of owning a house year after year (except, of course, in warm climates).

To be sure, there is more to comfort, and conversely to discomfort, than heating alone. The discomfort house is cursed with cold, hard-to-heat rooms in winter, but many also tend to have excessively dry air in winter, and come summer, the houses are often furnace-hot. The same things that cause a house to be chilly and cold often cause dry-air problems and excessive heat in summer. This is not true for all houses, but for many the basic causes are related (and so are the cures).

What Is True Comfort?

Ideally, to keep human beings comfortable in winter, the indoor temperature in a house should be maintained at about 72 degrees, uniformly in all rooms, and the relative humidity at 25 to 30 percent. These are the proven conditions for indoor comfort for most people in winter, according to extensive physiological tests sponsored by the American Society of Heating, Refrigerating, and Air-Conditioning Engineers, probably the country's foremost authority on the subject. Those conditions have been confirmed by actual experience in houses. If you must set your thermostat up to 75 degrees or higher, something is wrong (in addition to the fact that you're spending too much money for heat).

Some doctors, by the way, claim that the indoor relative humidity in a house should be maintained at 40 to 45 percent in winter for health reasons, which is exceedingly high indoor humidity in winter. Relative humidity that high is virtually impossible to maintain in a typical house in winter. Even if it could be done, the moisture would be so dense in the house that water would be streaming down the walls and windows, very likely causing serious structural damage to the house.

How do you avoid the discomfort house? How can you be sure that a house will be truly comfortable? How do you keep down the fuel bills? The answer is the same in each case. Put simply, the house should be properly insulated and properly heated. The rest of this chapter spells out what these two essential requirements are and how to check for each.

Top Priority for Comfort: Insulation

The most important cause of physical discomfort in a house is not poor heating; it is little or no insulation. Even the best, most expensive heating system can't keep you truly warm if you've

Classic photograph shows how double-pane insulating glass (left) does not frost up in winter. Twindow glass is used here. Glass at right is ordinary single-pane glass. (*Pittsburgh Plate Glass Company*)

been shortchanged on insulation. With little or no insulation, during cold weather the exterior walls, floors, and ceilings get quite cold. The heating thermostat can be turned up to 75 or even 80 degrees, and the house air may be that hot, but it won't help much. The cold surrounding surfaces will draw off excessive body heat from your skin (by radiation). You get goose pimples and feel chilled because body heat is drawn off faster than your blood can make it up. You feel cold for the same reason you feel chilled standing in front of an open refrigerator. The cold is drawing off too much body heat too fast. In addition, cold walls, windows, and ceilings set up drafts which swirl into your rooms. They are worst of all swirling down from an icy windowpane.

The cure is plenty of insulation. With insulation the house shell and its interior surfaces do not get so cold. Because they are kept warmer, body-heat loss to the surrounding house shell is reduced sharply. Cold drafts and little breezes do not swirl into the rooms. You're far more comfortable at about 72 degrees. The thermostat need not be raised way up (which is a little-known reason why insulation contributes to lower fuel costs).

Any skeptic who doubts the importance of insulation should know about a group of families who bought three-bedroom contemporary houses a few years ago about ten miles south of Minneapolis. These houses probably hold the all-time record for low-cost heating. Although winter temperatures of 20 degrees below zero are common there, we can testify as a result of visiting the houses that the houses are completely heated each year for a mere $85 to $90 a winter on the average. Yet the heating plant in each is the simplest kind of low-cost furnace. In addition, the houses have a wide expanse of floor-to-ceiling glass window-wall in each living room.

Not only are the heating bills so low, the houses are also remarkably warm and comfortable during winter. This is all because the builder, Robert Norsen, who is also an engineer, had the houses insulated from floor to roof with two to three times the usual insulation put in houses and used windows of double-glazed insulating glass. Norsen also located each house so the big living-room windows face south. They let a maximum amount of warm sunshine flood into the houses in winter, which helps heat the houses for nothing. The houses represent one of the finest examples of design for low-cost comfort we know of, as well as being a fine testimonial to the importance of good insulation.

Another accolade for insulation is the rock-bottom heating and air-conditioning bills in the houses built by a South Bend, Indiana, builder named Andy Place ($150 a year or less), as noted in Chapter 4. The secret? It's the same as Norsen's. Place's houses are thoroughly insulated according to the highest standards (given in a moment), including windows of double-glazed insulating glass.

Similar benefits are possible in nearly every climate zone of the country, according to a study of some eighty actual houses sponsored by the Owens-Corning Fiberglas Corporation. The study shows that a typical 1,250-square-foot house that is properly designed and insulated can be completely heated and centrally air-conditioned virtually anywhere in the United States for no more than $150 a year, all told. That's less than $14 a month, on the average, based on average fuel costs of ten cents a therm and cooling electricity at two cents a kilowatt hour. Again, the test houses were each insulated to the hilt. (In addition, cooling costs are kept down by such things as careful shading of big windows exposed to hot sunshine.)

How Much Insulation?

Consider a new house first. And for the moment forget about the brand and thickness of insulation used. The best test for adequate insulation is its R value, which stands for "resistance to heat flow." The higher the R value, the better it will prevent heat from leaking out of a house. It is a new grading standard that is now marked on many brands of insulation, though not all. The insulation you see in a new house should be marked according to the following standards:

Over the ceiling: This means the insulation at the attic floor or any other ceiling under a roof. Insulation here should be marked with at least an R-19 in the coldest climates and in any house anywhere that has electric heat or central air conditioning. This calls for mineral-wool insulation at least 5½ to 6½ inches thick. If there is electric heat, ratings of R-20 to R-24 are even better. If you are concerned with gas or oil heating only and will not have air conditioning, you can step down to an R-13, but it is best to accept nothing lower.

The walls: You need at least an R-11 for top comfort in a cold climate—that is, with or without electric heat or air conditioning— and an R-17 if the climate is not severe in winter or with gas or oil heat and no air conditioning. That will call for 2 to 3 inches of mineral-wool insulation thickness. Some people say, by the way, that wall insulation is unnecessary so long as the attic is insulated. That's poppycock, an old wives' tale. The best way to keep walls from getting icy cold is to pad them with insulation, and wall insulation also pays for itself in fuel savings.

The floors: The first floor of a house built over a crawl space— floor raised a few feet over the ground and no basement—should have R-11 insulation for best results. This can be cut a little for economy, but don't settle for less than R-7. You can tell what's there by crawling in under the floor and looking at the insulation.

A house with a concrete-slab floor on the ground and no basement should have edge insulation around the perimeter of the con-

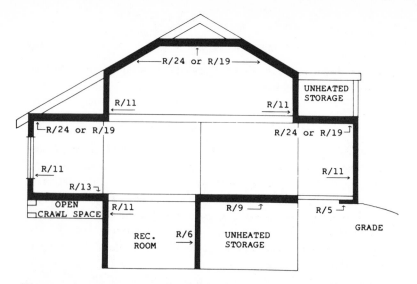

R/24 or R/19

R/11   R/11

UNHEATED STORAGE

R/24 or R/19   R/24 or R/19

R/11   R/11

R/13

OPEN CRAWL SPACE   R/11   R/9   R/5   GRADE

REC. ROOM   R/6   UNHEATED STORAGE

Diagram shows each part of a house that should be insulated and the insulation R value required. (*National Mineral Wool Insulation Association*)

Thick blanket of insulation over the ceiling will be five to seven inches thick for real summer and winter comfort. Black lining underneath insulation is asphalt-treated vapor barrier. (*National Mineral Wool Insulation Association*)

crete floor, its outside curb. This is rigid-board insulation made of either styrofoam or rigid mineral-wool sheets. For involved technical reasons edge insulation does not come marked with R values. Gauge it according to the thickness used. It should be at least 1½ to 2 inches, up to 3 inches in a very cold climate. You won't see it easily either, because properly installed, it is placed a foot or two inside the outer curb of the floor when the floor cement is poured, as noted in the accompanying diagram. Usually you must ask the builder if it is there and how much. Insulation is unnecessary under the whole cement floor because the ground below, sheltered from the weather by the house, does not get very cold.

Floor insulation in a house with a basement is usually unnecessary. Basements are usually warm enough to prevent cold floors.

Suppose the insulation in a house is not R-marked. This is not a good sign, even if the kind used appears to be ample. It may or may not be, and often is not. That's because, as already indicated, thickness alone is no guarantee of performance. The kind of material, its thickness, and what engineers call its k factor are the vital things. Some brands, including some well-known widely ad-

Diagrams show proper construction for a house with no basement. House built over a crawl space (left) should have: (1) vapor barrier over the ground, (2) vents to air the crawl space, (3) insulation under the floor. House with concrete floor over the ground (right) should have: (1) vapor barrier between the floor and the ground, (2) edge insulation around the perimeter of the floor to prevent excessive heat loss and cold floors.

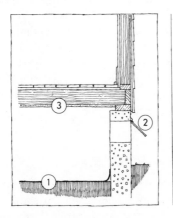
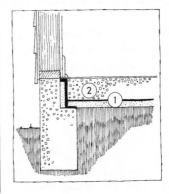

vertised products, have a notoriously low insulating ability. You may need eight or nine inches of thickness with one of them to give you the equivalent insulating effect of half that thickness with a really good brand. The only surefire test is R value.

We stress mineral-wool insulation. It's an inorganic material and therefore rot-proof and fire-resistant and unlikely to be eaten by bugs, mice, or rodents. We think it's the best all-around insulation. It has various generic names, such as glass wool, mineral wool, glass fiber, and fiberglass. Other insulation materials include wood fiber and cellulose fiber, both being organic materials that require chemical treatment. There is also aluminum-foil insulation, which we do not recommend for houses in a cold climate (except for the floor of a crawl-space house and only then if it conforms to the minimum R-value standards noted). Regular insulation bats and blankets are sometimes sold with an aluminum-foil skin, which is something else again. It can be fine providing it meets the R-value standards.

There is also loose-fill insulation which you may see loosely blown into the walls or over the ceiling of a house. It is widely used because it is cheaper than bat or blanket insulation. Because it, too, does not come with an R value, its thickness should be equivalent to those given with the R-value standards.

Vapor Barriers

Virtually every house in every climate should be lined with a vapor barrier to prevent serious moisture damage to the structure. A vapor barrier can be seen as a black asphalt or aluminum-foil cover integral with the insulation used, or it may be a polyethylene plastic membrane lining the house shell. It should usually go between the insulation and the inside of the house. A vapor barrier is also essential under the concrete floor of a slab-on-ground house. It is usually a large sheet of polyethelene plastic laid over the ground bed before the cement is poured.

Is an Old House Insulated?

It's easy to check for ceiling insulation or the lack of it in an old house. Go up to the attic and look. The insulation should be between the beams at the attic floor. If it is installed overhead between the sloping roof rafters directly under the roof, it does not do much good. If there are rooms in the attic, their walls and ceilings should be padded with thick insulation that meets the R-value standards for walls and ceilings (or has the equivalent thickness). R values are not likely on insulation in many used houses because they were not introduced until the early 1960's. You will usually have to fall back on the thickness used for an indication of its adequacy.

Determining the presence of wall insulation is harder, if not impossible. While in the attic you may be able to see down into the cavities of the outer walls, or from the basement look up into them. If you cannot see because of obstructions, another way may be possible. It is a touch test that will work if the weather is cold and the heating is on. Inside the house put the palm of your hand flat against the exterior walls in several rooms, especially the walls on the north. The walls should feel as warm to the touch, or almost so, as an interior wall in the middle of the house. If the outside wall is cold or downright chilly to the touch, there's little or no insulation. Excessive heat is leaking out. (Try the same test during cold weather on your present house. It can be quite revealing.)

Use the palm test also to check for floor insulation in a house with no basement. Do it at the outer perimeter on the floor—in other words, near the exterior walls. If the floor there is cold, there's little or no insulation. The palm test will not work during mild or warm weather, and you must rely on the owner's word when you ask if the house is insulated.

The age of a house can also indicate the presence or lack of insulation, since insulation generally was not put in houses built before the late 1940's. A house built earlier will lack it, particularly in the walls, unless, of course, the owner had it put in.

Cost of Insulating an Old House

If a house you are buying needs insulation, the walls can usually be opened up on the outside and woolly insulation blown in. The cost installed will range from about 20 to 30 cents per square foot of wall. It usually costs about $500 to $1,000 for the average house. It also can be blown into the attic, but putting down bats or blankets of insulation at the attic floor is better. Cost of either will range from about 8 to 15 cents per square foot, or roughly $80 to $150 per one thousand square feet of attic floor. New two-to-three-inch-thick edge insulation for the perimeter of a concrete floor slab will cost approximately 25 cents per square foot, or roughly 50 cents per foot of floor perimeter. For a 24- by 40-foot house, thus about 130 feet of concrete curb to be insulated, cost would therefore run about $65, plus installation. The cost of insulating the floor of a crawl-space house will run about 8 to 14 cents per square foot, depending on the labor required.

Door and Window Insulation

Storm doors and windows are virtually essential for comfort in a cold climate and will cut your fuel bills, too. Because they are not usually given with a new house, you have to buy them. Cost for good-quality storm windows runs at least $25 to $35 apiece; $80 to $95 apiece for good storm doors. At that price it can be worth your while to have the builder install double-glazed Thermopane or comparable insulating glass at least for picture windows and windows exposed to the biting lash of northerly winds. Also check for the presence of weather stripping on windows and doors, as noted in Chapter 8. It's the best way to stop cold air from whistling into the house.

The Heating System

There is forced-warm-air heat, the most widely used nowadays; hot-water heat ("hydronic," which includes radiant floor heat); and electric heat. These are the three main kinds of central heating. Each can heat perfectly well *provided* it is installed right. There are no intrinsic drawbacks to any one of the three. Sometimes marginal equipment is used, but most times problems that arise are the result of poor installation.

Forced-Warm-Air Heat

There is a furnace with a blower that sends heated air through ducts to the rooms of the house. The air ducts are its telltale sign. Probably its biggest advantage is that it can be economically teamed up with central air conditioning, the same ducts being used for both heating and cooling. A warm-air system can be fueled by either gas or oil or powered by electricity. An electric furnace has electric heating elements inside, rather than a fuel-burning heat chamber.

There is also the old-fashioned gravity circulating warm-air system which you will see in some old houses. There's no blower; the heated air, being lighter, rises slowly from the furnace up to the house through large octopuslike ducts emanating from the furnace. It usually means inferior heating. Eventually a forced-warm-air furnace and new ductwork will be needed.

The quality of a warm-air system depends on the kind of furnace and how well the vital ducts are designed. Look for a furnace with a ten-year warranty (on its important combustion chamber) and a pulley-driven blower. This is the better "custom" kind, costing only 5 to 10 percent more than the marginal "builder" or "economy" kind. Take off the front panel, and see if the blower is driven by a rubber pulley, like an automobile fan belt. It connects the blower to the electric motor that drives it. If there is no pulley and the blower is connected directly to its motor (same shaft for both), it is almost always the sign of an economy furnace with a one-year warranty only. Don't go by the brand, since even the best manufacturers sell both kinds.

The duct system, which is crucial for efficient heat supply and uniform temperatures, should be what engineers call a perimeter design. The warm-air outlets in the rooms should be located in the floor or at wall baseboard level, and most important, they should be located around the *exterior* perimeter of the house, preferably under windows. The purpose is to supply the heat at the source of the greatest cold—the exterior walls and windows. Usually at least one outlet should be located at each exterior wall in a room. Two or more are often needed in large rooms or along extended walls under long picture windows. You want a curtain of warm air thrown up from the registers around the perimeter of the house between you and the outside cold.

Perimeter heating is virtually mandatory for good warm-air heating in a cold climate, especially in a house without a basement. It is not so important, however, in a warm climate. The kind of warm-air system that's not very efficient is one with the

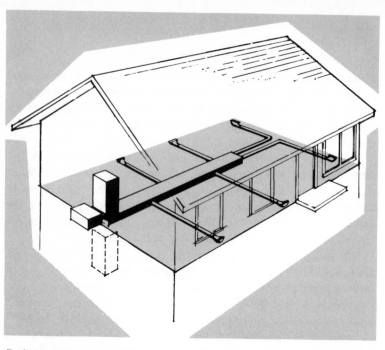

Perimeter heat distribution is a must for comfort with warm-air heat, except in the warmest climates. Warm air from furnace is channeled through ducts to outlets in the floor or baseboard at exterior wall location. (*Illustration courtesy* Better Homes & Gardens, © *Meredith Corporation, 1963*)

supply outlets, the registers, located in the interior walls or at ceiling level. This kind of design by and large works well only in a mild winter climate.

Check the way the main ducts are attached to the furnace. Metal ducts should not be attached directly to the furnace because that will let noise and vibration from the furnace spread through the ducts. The ducts should be coupled to the furnace by a short canvas collar that absorbs furnace vibration and noise. This is also a good indication of the quality of the rest of the heating system—that is, a canvas collar may indicate good design throughout.

If a house has two or more floor levels or is a long, spread-out ranch, it should generally have separate heating zones. This calls for separate thermostats that permit individual heat control for each zone. That's the way to get uniform temperature control and prevent some rooms from getting too hot while others are too cold.

Zone controls are also needed for such houses with hot-water heat. If it's a new house, also say that you want the warm-air system adjusted for what engineers call Continuous Air Circulation, or C.A.C. The blower is set to run all the time, not just when heat is required, thus giving constant air circulation. More uniform temperature control results, hence greater comfort. If it's an old house, a heating man can do this for you, unless it's already so adjusted. Finally, your best guarantee of good warm-air heating is a Silver Shield system, which is one that has been designed and installed according to the stiff standards of the National Warm Air Heating & Air Conditioning Association.

Hot-Water (Hydronic) Heat

Water is heated in a central boiler and flows to room radiators. The best kind is a forced circulating system which has a pump next to the boiler to push the water around. There are cast-iron and steel boilers. A cast-iron one is far more rugged and dependable and is usually guaranteed for at least twenty years. It should show an IBR seal on its nameplate, which means it conforms with the design standards of the Institute of Boiler and Radiator Manufacturers.

A steel boiler can be adequate in an area with soft water; if the local water supply is hard and corrosive, it should be shunned like the plague. A good steel boiler will display on its nameplate an SBI seal (Steel Boiler Institute).

There should be enough radiators around the exterior walls. What is enough? This is tough to answer because it varies from house to house. There are no set rules. Do look for at least one radiator below each exposed wall of a room, and more than one for long wall exposures.

The best radiators are the long, low, baseboard kind, which are about six to ten inches high and as much as ten feet long, sometimes longer. They are usually made with copper or aluminum heating fins. They are sometimes difficult to clean, though, and may be noisy when the heat goes on or off. There are also cast-iron baseboard radiators, the elite kind; but they are expensive and you will generally see them only in the very best houses.

New baseboard radiator for hot-water heat is obviously an aesthetic improvement, compared with old-fashioned radiators. The slender baseboard kind also spreads heat more uniformly and is a more effective counter heat force to cold drafts falling down from window. (*Better Heating-Cooling Council*)

If a house has hot-water radiant floor heat, tread warily. Hot water circulates through pipes embedded in the floor, usually of concrete, and the floor acts as a heating panel for the house, like a low-temperature hot plate. There are some perfectly good radiant systems, but unfortunately many more poor ones, because they are hard to design and install properly. If a pipe breaks, the floor has to be dug up. Another drawback of radiant heat is sluggish operation. The whole floor has to heat up before you get heat. This can take an hour or two. It's best to avoid radiant heat unless you are assured that it has been properly installed.

Electric Heat

There are two crucial prerequisites for efficient electric heat: (1) the house must be very well insulated, and (2) the local cost of electricity must be low enough to make it feasible. Don't compromise on either point.

The insulation should conform to the highest R standards in an electrically heated house. Even more insulation (such as eight to nine inches thickness at the attic floor) will be welcome in a really cold climate. Storm windows and doors are also essential to keep down the heat loss and thus the electricity consumption.

The local electric rate for heating should be no more than about 1.5 cents per kilowatt hour and preferably 1 cent or less. It should be about 1 cent or less if your bills are to be no higher than they would be with gas or oil. A 1-cent-per-kilowatt-hour rate, more or less, will give heating bills at the same level as gas heat at about 12 cents per therm and oil at 15 cents per gallon.

Electric heat has undeniable advantages: no fuel burned, no furnace or boiler to service, repair, or replace, plus individual thermostats for each room (optional), and the lowest initial installation cost. As a result, you may be willing to pay a little more for operation. You may like it even if the local electric rate runs as high as 1.5 cents per kilowatt hour.

Be a little wary of it in a new house. Some builders use it chiefly because of the low initial cost, even though the local power rates are higher than they should be for economical operation. Get an estimate of the annual heating bills directly from the local electric utility. Some utilities will guarantee that the heating bills will not exceed a given figure. Then you need not worry. In an old house the electric bills for heating should be produced by the seller for your inspection.

Electric heat is coming up strong, though it has still not proved itself in some parts of the country, because some contractors are only just learning about it. When you check the installation, each of the electric-heat room radiators (convectors) should carry the UL seal of the Underwriters' Laboratories. The systems should be installed according to the standards of the National Electrical Manufacturers Association. Your sales-contract specifications should say this. If baseboard heating convectors are used, look for medium-density models, which are good, or low-density ones, the best. The high-density kind are the cheapest in quality and performance.

Gas versus Oil Heat

Which fuel is cheaper—gas or oil? It depends on the relative price of each in your area. Gas rates vary across the nation from as little as six cents a therm to over fifteen cents a therm. A therm gives you 100,000 Btu's (British thermal units) of heat. Gas heat, therefore, can cost up to two to three times as much for a house in a high-cost gas territory, compared with the same amount of gas burned to heat a house in a low-cost territory. Oil, on the other hand, generally costs in the neighborhood of eighteen cents a gallon, give or take a few cents.

Thus the key to economical gas heat hinges on your local utility gas rate in comparison with the cost of oil. Gas will be competitive with eighteen-cent oil at a local rate of about fourteen cents per therm for gas. The exact competitive level for equality depends on such things as the house size, the amount of insulation, and the efficiency of the particular heating plant in the house. Gas will have the edge over oil if it costs that much or less.

To determine the relative economy of gas versus oil and also one or the other versus electric heat, call the local gas utility for their gas heating rate. Frankly ask one of their engineers if gas is cheaper or more expensive. You'll usually get a straight answer from a knowledgeable man at the utility. To double-check, call a few heating contractors who handle both. Another indication of the cheapest heating power is the most popular kind in the area.

Gas heat costs less to install initially than oil (partly because no fuel tank is required), and in general it requires less service and maintenance than oil. Remember that both warm-air and hot-water heating units may be fueled by either; the only difference is the type of fuel combustion. An oil-fired unit almost always requires cleaning and readjustment every year (to maintain high-efficiency operation), whereas gas units can go for years with no servicing. As far as cleanliness goes, don't believe the wild advertising claims made by the proponents of different fuels. A modern gas or oil unit, properly installed, will spread virtually no dirt or soot. An older system, however, and particularly the dirty old obsolete oil burners found in some used houses, are something else again. They can be the devil's own for spreading oily soot. In an old house you'll probably want that kind of relic replaced. Cost will run about $200 to $250 if just the burner mechanism is to be replaced; $500 to $1,000 if the whole heating unit must be replaced.

Is the Heating System Large Enough?

The heating in a house should be guaranteed to maintain 70 degrees or better indoors when the temperature outdoors is coldest in winter. In Chicago that means 5 degrees below zero outdoors; in New York, 0 degrees. In International Falls, Minnesota—one of the coldest cities in the country—it's 30 degrees below zero, which is the outside temperature that a house heating plant there should be designed to cope with.

Less heating capacity is required in the South, of course. A furnace in New Orleans, for example, needs only enough heating capacity to maintain 70 degrees indoors when it is 30 degrees above zero outdoors, the coldest weather generally encountered there. The sales contract for a house should contain that kind of guarantee, citing the minimum winter temperature for the climate at which the house heater will keep you warm.

The equipment's heating capacity will be noted on the name-plate in Btu's per hour. One Btu is roughly the amount of heat given off by an old-fashioned wooden match. Technically, it is the heat required to raise the temperature of one pound of water by one degree Fahrenheit. A typical $30,000 house will ordinarily need a heater with a capacity of from 75,000 to 125,000 Btu's per hour, the exact amount depending on the construction, amount of insulation, and climate zone.

In a northern climate with an outdoor design temperature of zero degrees a house of average construction will have what engineers call a heat loss of about 50 Btu's per square foot of heated living area. A 1,500-square-foot house, therefore, will have a total heat loss of 75,000 Btu's (50 times 1,500). The heating unit should be that large to counteract the heat loss and keep the house up to 70 degrees. That's how the heater is sized. Figuring the heat loss, however, requires a computation that takes into account the thermal characteristics of the walls, windows, roof, and everything else that bears on the heat flow from inside the structure to out.

A house with really good insulation plus storm windows will have less heat loss, down to around 30 Btu's per square foot of floor area. Thus a 30-Btu-per-square-foot heat loss for a 1,500-square-foot house will require a heating unit with only 45,000 Btu's per hour of capacity. That's the way a house should be built for electric heat or for really low-cost heating with any other fuel. It also shows how spending a little extra money for more insulation (which is cheap) brings about savings on the heating plant, which can be a smaller size.

You can make an approximate check on the heating capacity in a house, therefore, by figuring the total living area in square feet. Assuming average construction in a northern climate, multiply that figure by 50 Btu's per square foot. A 2,000-square-foot house, for example, should have 100,000 Btu's of heating capacity (2,000 by 50). The heating unit should be marked with that capacity or a little more on its nameplate. An old house with drafty windows and little or no insulation may require 60 Btu's per square foot; a newer house with good insulation and storm windows will need 40 to 50. You will have to weigh the Btu's needed per square foot according to whether or not the climate is warmer or colder than the average in the North.

Dry-Air Discomfort

How do you maintain the right relative humidity in a house for health and comfort? The kind of heating has less to do with it than you may think. It is often said that warm-air heat, for example, is "dry heat." This is not true. Keeping the moisture at a good level in winter depends far more on the house construction. The air in loosely built old houses tends to get excessively dry in winter because of the cracks and many little leaks in the structure. The moisture inside is drawn out inexorably as a result of the sharp difference between the vapor pressure indoors and out. In winter it is usually very low outdoors.

A new tightly built house, however, retains much of its natural moisture, particularly if it is well insulated and sealed with vapor barriers. Scientific studies at Purdue University show that enough moisture for adequate indoor humidity is generated in a house as a result of family activities like cooking, washing, bathing, and so on. If the house is comparatively tight, the odds are good that you won't suffer from dry air. The moisture is kept in, and the air will not get excessively dry. Your best assurance for comfortable humidity conditions is a tightly built, well-insulated house structure.

If you buy an old house with a dry-air problem in winter, the problem may be alleviated by storm windows, storm doors, and insulation. If not, you must add a humidifying device, which for a whole house will cost about $150 to $250. Sometimes you may need only a small vaporizer at your bedside at night, which is when the air is driest (because it is coldest).

If you buy a superinsulated house with electric heat, the reverse condition—too much indoor moisture—can be a problem. Sometimes there's so much moisture, it will literally stream down the walls. Little of it can get outdoors because the house is so tight. This can be prevented with a kitchen exhaust fan wired to a humidistat control, which should be a mandatory device in houses with electric heat. Should the humidity level get too high, the humidistat automatically turns on the fan to get rid of the excess vapor. The humidistat is preset at 25-to-30-percent relative humidity, or whatever you find by experiment is needed. An exhaust fan in each bathroom is recommended, though not always essential.

Summer Comfort and Air Conditioning

No question about it, not only is air conditioning the way to keep cool in summer, but central air conditioning has arrived for houses. By the beginning of the 1970's close to one million central systems were being installed in houses (new and old) a year, and the number was still climbing. About 30 percent of all new houses were being equipped with it, with that figure steadily climbing, too.

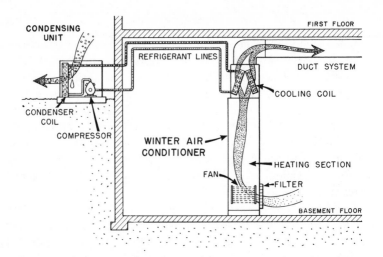

Diagram shows popular method of combining central air conditioning with warm-air heating. The cooling-coil section on top of the furnace (winter air conditioner) is connected to the outdoor condenser unit with copper refrigerant piping. Condensing unit goes outside for access to outdoor air; this also puts operating noise outside the house. (*Carrier Corporation*)

What's more, its price has come down sharply, and its operating cost has turned out to be surprisingly low in most houses.

Air conditioning is fast becoming a necessity and no longer a luxury in houses. It is also growing more important for maintaining the resale value of houses. It has come on much like the advent of central heat around the turn of the twentieth century, and it promises to influence the way houses are built and the way we live as much in its way as central heat did. Any skeptic who doubts this should go back to the records of the early 1900's, when central heat was kicking up a storm of controversy. In 1906 a well-known ladies' magazine of the time (still a major magazine) blasted that newfangled device, the whole-house furnace, "with its forbidding installation cost." It cried that the potbellied coal stove was as fine a room heater as anyone could ask for. (The same magazine was also skeptical of another newcomer in houses, electricity, and was cautioning its readers that "electricity is convenient but gaslight is still the best buy at seven times less cost. . . .")

Clearly, if you are buying a new house, equipping it with central air conditioning can make sense in all but the mildest summer climates. Its initial cost for the average new house will range as low as $750, sometimes less, up to about $1,350. That's for combining it with forced-warm-air heat and for two to three "tons" of air conditioning. A ton is equal to 12,000 Btu's of cooling capacity (not a ton of weight). It gives you the equivalent cooling effect of that given off in one hour by a block of ice weighing one ton. The initial cost will be somewhat higher in a house with hot-water or conventional electric heat, because new ducts must be put in for the cooling. The better the house is designed for air conditioning and the more insulation it has, the less cooling capacity is needed and the lower, therefore, the air-conditioning cost.

Future Cooling Insurance

The price of adding central air conditioning to an existing house can run considerably more than in a new house (because of breaking through walls, altering the heating, and so on). You may pass up air conditioning in a new house you buy because you feel you can always add it later. This can be an expensive mistake. It need not be a mistake if you have a new house equipped with a few low-cost provisions that will make possible the installation of central cooling any time later at a low price.

Tell the builder or the heating contractor that you want heating ducts that will accommodate central air conditioning, too. Cooling usually requires bigger ducts. The furnace chosen should be one with a blower large enough for cooling, one designed to accept air conditioning. Some automatically are; others are not. A special compartment (plenum) should be provided, usually above the furnace, where the cooling coil can be easily inserted at the proper time. The electrical wiring board should have a spare 240-volt circuit to handle the air conditioner. If the supply air ducts pass through a room or space that will not be air-conditioned, like the garage or a crawl space, the ducts require insulation. Ducts in the basement, however, ordinarily need not be insulated for air conditioning. These stitch-in-time provisions for cooling should cost no more than about $50 initially, but they can reduce

This New England house clearly illustrates how different sections (zones) of a house can be subject to different weather exposures. As a result, the heating needs vary throughout the house, and a zoned heating system is required to provide uniform temperature control indoors. (*Edison Electric Institute*)

the expense of installing air conditioning later by ten times that amount. The money spent is good insurance.

How Much Air Conditioning?

If air conditioning is already in a new or an old house you may buy, is there enough for the house? It should be guaranteed to maintain the house at 75 degrees and 50-percent relative humidity indoors when the outside weather is at its worst. That means an outdoor design temperature of 95 degrees in most northern cities like New York and Chicago, and 95 degrees also in certain southern cities like Houston, New Orleans, and Miami. It may get more muggy and humid in those southern cities, but not necessarily hotter. In other southern cities, like Tulsa, Dallas, and Phoenix, the outdoor design temperature in summer ranges from 100 to 105 degrees; thus, more cooling capacity and larger units are required to keep a house at 75 degrees.

A typical house of around 1,500 square feet of floor area in cities with a 95-degree summer peak heat usually requires about two or three tons of cooling capacity. Larger units are required in a city with hotter summer weather. As with heating, it is impossible to give general rules on how much cooling is required for different houses. The capacity for each must be computed separately. You should, however, request that the builder or seller guarantee that the air conditioning will provide adequate comfort—75 degrees and no more than 50-percent relative humidity indoors—during the hottest days of summer.

Air-Conditioning Operating Cost

A typical house in the $25,000 to $35,000 price range can be fully air-conditioned in the North for $60 to $85 over the whole summer. That's $20 to $28 a month for three months of central cooling. In the hot South bills for the same kind of houses range from about $75 to $135 a summer, or up to $27 a month on the average for five months of cooling. These figures are based on actual bills from typical houses, with electrical rates averaging 2 cents per kilowatt hour.

Bills will run even lower for well-insulated houses and houses that are designed to keep down cooling bills (by shading big windows, for example), as we have already indicated. Conversely, they may run somewhat higher for a loosely built old house, though that isn't always true. I know of a rather large (2,000 square feet) old Victorian house in a New York suburb that was built in 1894 and insulated and equipped with central air conditioning in 1960. The cost of air-conditioning it averages between $65 and $70 a summer (with 2.3-cent electricity), or less than $25 a month. (I owned it for ten years and paid the bills.)

The Heat Pump

The heat pump is a summer-winter air conditioner, a piece of equipment that supplies warm *or* cool air to a house with a refrigeration compressor. In summer it works like a regular air conditioner. In winter the refrigeration cycle is reversed, and it plucks heat from the outside air and delivers it inside. Because electricity is used, it means electric heat. A house with a heat pump, therefore, must be insulated to the hilt, as must any other electrically heated house.

Most brands of heat pumps, however, work better in the warm South than in the cold North. Because of technical problems with the heating cycle, many heat pumps have still not been refined for trouble-free operation in the North. These problems may be solved in the future, but until they are, it is best to be wary of a heat pump in a cold climate.

Air-Conditioning Summary

By all means consider air conditioning when you buy a house. To play safe, look for a top-brand name, such as Carrier, York, or Lennox. The ability of the installing dealer or contractor is all-important, too. He should be a man who is well established locally and has a good reputation for service. With a new house get an estimate of the cost of operation as well as a guarantee on performance. With an old house ask to see past summer electric bills.

Comfort Summary

The number-one, most widespread cause of discomfort in a house is little or no insulation. Wrapping a house in a good blanket of insulation can compensate for many a heating deficiency. That includes, of course, storm doors and windows and weather stripping. The next cause, to be sure, is poor heating. By and large, poor heating stems more from a poor installation—a poor heating *system*—than it does from a cheap heating unit per se.

So if you buy a new house, have it insulated to the hilt. Also be sure the heating is installed properly, particularly with warm-air heat (which calls for perimeter ducts in most climate zones and plenty of heating outlets). If you buy an existing house, check first in the insulation. If there is not enough, make sure more can be added. If a new heating plant is needed, it will generally cost from about $600 to $1,000, depending on the size needed and how much upgrading the rest of the system needs.

Remember that central air conditioning can be a plus factor. We've noted its cost in typical new houses; to add it to an existing house, increase the installed cost given by 20 to 50 percent.

The Gimmick
House

A young couple we know bought a $34,500 house in a new development we'll call Highway Acres. But why did they buy that particular house in that particular development?

They bought it, of all things, principally because of a luminous Japanese ceiling in the downstairs bathroom. It was a distinctive, eye-catching feature, a suspended light screen illuminated by recessed lights above. What's more, it turned out later that more than half of the buyers of the eighty houses in Highway Acres also bought their houses largely because of the luminous ceiling feature in the one bathroom.

That's not unique, either. Surveys show that many houses are bought because of one or more distinctive features that trigger the buying impulse. The trouble is that such features are sometimes gimmicks, put there deliberately to catch the eye of buyers, in the same way that tail fins a few years ago were designed to sell cars (which they did by the millions) and eye-catching new packaging gimmicks flooding supermarket shelves are designed to trigger the buying impulse.

What the Gimmick House Is

There's nothing basically wrong in a manufacturer's putting his best foot forward and making his product distinctive and attractive, thus more salable. But what is culpable are the gimmicks used to trick us into buying a product that is made to appear better than it actually is. The dictionary defines the word "gimmick" as "an attention-catching device, a novel twist, or a gadget. . . ."

Borrowing from that definition, we call the gimmick house a house with one or more special features that *seem* to make the whole house special, though this is not necessarily so. The houses in Highway Acres are marginal house traps, as many a buyer there has since found out. Measured against any real standards, they are of execrable design. The interior floor plan in most is a nightmare for living. The kitchens are singularly small and badly planned, and the construction is of marginal if not of downright shoddy quality. Yet the irresistible appeal of the Japanese ceiling so overshadowed the flaws that the builder sold some $2 million worth of marginal houses at an extra cost of about $65 per house (the estimated cost of the glamour ceilings), which was not a bad investment.

Why did the Japanese ceiling trigger so many buying impulses? We don't know for sure, but what we were told may be a large part of the answer (as well as shedding light on how to avoid the gimmick-house trap). One of the buyers and present owners told us, "The ceiling was distinctive. My wife and I liked it at once. We liked the Japanese styling. Most of all, I think, it gave us confidence in the house. We felt that if the builder put something extra like that into the house, he probably took pains with the rest of the house. It made us feel that the whole house was especially well built."

The gimmicks used to sell houses take a variety of shapes and forms. They include fancy kitchen trappings like a dining-room pass-through wall, a shiny new wall oven, or an appliance plug-in center—all, in themselves, desirable additions—intercom systems,

Decorative ceiling lighting like this may add a little interest, but it doesn't necessarily enhance the intrinsic design of a house. Sometimes such features are nothing more than eye-catching gimmicks deliberately installed to provide an illusion of value when no real value exists. On the other hand, a roof skylight like the one shown here often does add genuine value.

showy fireplaces, wrought-iron balcony rails, roof pagodas, and so on. On a broader scale there are also design gimmicks, such as the "raised ranch," the "Colonial ranch," and the "split ranch." There has also been the "atrium house," a house with an interior court (which can be a splendid plan if carried off well). Each of these is a gimmick when it is built principally to sell the house irrespective of how well the house itself is designed and built.

To be sure, gimmicks can sometimes be perfectly functional and nice to have. The gimmick house is a trap to avoid, however, when one or two eye-catching features propel an unsuspecting couple into buying a house that they otherwise would not touch with a ten-foot pole. Are the house and its overall design and construction good, and is the house right for you and your family? Those are the key questions.

Home-Buying Motivations

The subject of the gimmick house also raises an important question: Why do people buy houses? More to the point, why do people buy a particular kind of house? Certain strong emotional forces come into play when people buy houses. Much is still unknown about our motivations, though various studies have been made to find out. What has been learned can be instructive in defining your reasons for buying a house, as well as in helping you avoid the gimmick house trap. Builders and real-estate brokers continually search for the answers in order to find out how to sell more houses. It's time the home-buyer understood some of the forces at work, too!

Ask the typical home-buyer why he seeks a new house, and according to the usual superficial studies, he'll say he wants more living space and bigger and better living quarters. Others want a little property of their own. But such reasons are only the beginning. According to a study by Cornell University researchers, some people buy houses chiefly for status and prestige reasons.

Others buy a house chiefly because it's a financial investment that will grow in value. Still other people most of all want a house that will best fulfill the personal needs of their families, with special emphasis on benefits for growing children (such as ample playing space and a location near good schools).

Scratch a little more, however, and we also learn that our houses tap wells of deep personal and psychological meaning to people. Most of us have known persons who take great pride in their homes. This is particularly true of women. The high importance of a house to a woman is indicated by a psychiatrist, Dr. Milton R. Sapirstein, in his book *Paradoxes of Everyday Life*. He says, "Ask any thoughtful person the crucial situations in a woman's life—the crisis points—and he would undoubtedly cite marriage, childbirth, menopause, and the loss of a beloved person." These are "the classic stress-producing experiences, the occasions that try women's souls. But there is a special experience which ranks at the top of the list in its capacity to precipitate emotional disorders. Observations . . . lead me to believe that there is no time at which a woman is more apt to go to pieces than when she is engaged in decorating her home."

Many women, of course, begin thinking of the decorating potential from the moment they first walk into a house for sale. Women are far less concerned with construction features, and understandably so. They are far more concerned with the value of a house in terms of the kind of home it will be for themselves and their families.

It is the man in the family, to be sure, who puts great importance on the structural bones of a house. Most men will walk down in the basement and check the furnace, climb into the attic for a look around, and peer into corners to size up the kind of two-by-fours used, even though many men don't know the difference between a furnace and a boiler or between No. 1 clear hardwood and ordinary hardboard.

A good many men are also sharply motivated by the financial aspects of a house and such things as its resale value. Once a house is purchased, some men derive great pleasure each month by opening up their mortgage-payment book and noting the increased equity being built up in their houses following each monthly payment. That, too, is understandable.

There is also the man who cannot bear the emotional burden of a mortgage. He cannot face up to buying and owning a house. Renting is much easier, even though buying and owning is almost always cheaper. The wives of such men, being women, usually pine for a home of their own. The husband requires great and long persuasion before he will break through his emotional block and finally consent to buying a house. Sometimes he never does. One woman in a southern city says, "It took us four months to buy a house once we started looking. But first it took me seven years to talk my husband into it!"

New versus Old Houses

Surveys show that home-buyers belong in two categories—those who prefer new houses and those who prefer the old. People who seek a new house place great importance on having a house that is new and up to date. They are quoted in surveys as saying, "We want a place that is modern, new, and clean." These words crop up in interviews again and again.

In the 1950's the ranch house was the newest style in houses, and as a result it was bought by the hundreds of thousands, if not by the millions. Then came the era of the split-level house. Split levels were bought by droves of house-buyers because they were new and different, regardless of how well, or how badly, they were designed and built. Since then we have noted the introduction of houses like the split-entry, the raised ranch, and the atrium house. Builders know that each holds irresistible appeal to many home-buyers, because each is supposed to be the very latest fashion in houses. Some people apparently do not realize that there are good atriums and bad ones, and just because a house is a new style doesn't mean that it is an especially good house.

Another study of home-buyers in a midwestern suburb showed that the kind of house was irrelevant as long as it was located in an area of new houses. This is particularly true for many young married people. They seek houses in a large *new* development, because they want to live among other young couples like themselves. They want to live where they can easily make friends with neighbors who are also starting out in life with common interests and young children like themselves. They fear, subconsciously perhaps, that buying a house in an older, established neighborhood would confront them with a difficult social situation. They are afraid, often rightly, that they and their children would be socially snubbed by the old-timers and neighbors around. It would be harder to make friends. They therefore head for new developments where everybody is starting out. The type of house is of secondary concern.

People who seek old houses do so for different reasons, too. Many are attracted to old houses by emotional forces as strong as those in people who seek new houses. They include persons who are, to be blunt, snobs who would not be caught dead in a new house development (but are sometimes caught financially dead by an old-house lemon). It includes others who have an honest wish for an old house with charm and tradition, sometimes because of their happy memories of growing up in a splendid old house. They want to repeat the pleasure they had with their parents, doing it again with their children. Still others seek social and/or business prestige that they feel they can obtain only by buying a large old house in an old, long-established neighborhood.

Important Features That Count

Once a home-seeker settles on an area he likes, he tends to search for a house that contains specific features that he sorely misses in his present house or apartment, according to a notable study, *What Makes the Home Buyer Tick?* by the late Pierre Martineau, who headed a market research group for the Chicago *Tribune*. The features sought may be a fully equipped modern kitchen, extra bedrooms, and plenty of storage and yard space as well as insulation and a good heating system.

Some buyers, on the other hand, don't know exactly what they want until they are struck by certain features they see in houses that remind them of drastic shortcomings in their existing homes or apartments. Then their search for a house narrows down to one with special features that assume paramount importance to them. And once a couple recognizes the availability of new features and modern conveniences lacking in their present home, their dissatisfaction grows sharply, Martineau said. Their search for a house is spurred on in an "intensive frenzied" way.

This is also the time when a sales gimmick can hit them with great impact and exert enormous influence on the decision to buy a house, even though the feature is nothing special and even though the particular house is of no great distinction. Martineau pointed out that it may be a distinctive fireplace, a winding staircase, a separate dining room. Sometimes it is merely a smart-looking cowling on the heating furnace, giving the impression that it is an outstanding heating system. The buyer infers that the rest of the house also must be outstanding. That does it. Whether it is a gimmick or not, a husband and wife, already on the verge of buying, buy.

Actually both husband and wife have probably given much thought to the house. They may not have checked it with an educated eye, but no glaring flaws have come to their attention. They are emotionally set up. Almost any distinctive feature—or any gimmick—will at this very moment serve to trigger the purchase. The special feature they see at this moment is final confirmation that this is the house for them. They buy it.

The Moment of Truth

Is it really a good house? Is it one that the buyers will truly be satisfied with? Let's take stock of what researchers have found out about our home-buying motives. They can tell us about how to buy a house and, among other things, how to avoid the gimmick house. The time to take stock of your home-buying motives, of course, is before reaching that final stage when, being human, you find yourself caught up by momentum. You've looked at so many houses for so long that all you want to do is buy a house, almost any house, and get it over with.

A few things should be clear. What kind of house do you really want, and why? Get rid of preconceived ideas you may have about houses before you shop for a house. You may think you want only a new house or nothing but an old house. Whichever it is, you should have valid reasons for your choice. Some people simply want a house that will require a minimum of upkeep and maintenance and therefore justifiably want a new house. There's nothing wrong with that, but you should be reminded that some new houses come with drastic built-in defects. You should know now, however, about that kind of new house. Those who lean strongly toward an old house should accept one at its own terms, realizing that among other things the old-house lemon should certainly be avoided. You know now about that breed, too.

You need not be ruthlessly objective and totally unemotional about buying a house. Respect the idea that the purchase of a house should be done with a realistic, hardheaded attitude. Nonetheless, one of the best tests for buying a house is how you *feel* about the house. In fact, many a bad home-buying decision could have been averted had the buyers, husband and wife, paused before buying to probe their bedrock buying motives. What kind of a house do they really want? Where do they really want to live? And do they truly feel they have found a good house?

Also remember that there is no perfect house. It does not exist. But if you feel confident that you have found a good house at a good price, it is usually one that should cause you no regrets.

Buying a house is a fairly important thing in our lives. Its importance is summed up by Sir Winston Churchill's piercing comment that first "we shape our buildings and afterward our buildings shape us."

Buying and owning a really good, trouble-free house can be a never-ending source of great pleasure and satisfaction.

Checklist for Buying a House

Here is a review of the main points in this book to help you when you shop for a house and also to make a final check on a house that you are ready to buy. Remember, though, that practically no house will be perfect and that some of the best houses may be deficient here and there. That's to be expected. On the other hand, if a house scores low on numerous checklist items, you have fair warning that it is probably a bad house.

The High-Priced House

- What is the fair market value of the house? Was this determined by a real-estate appraiser? How does it compare with the sales price?
- Does the house conform in price with comparable houses in the same area?
- Is the house located in a residential neighborhood that will

retain its character and value, if not increase in desirability? Or is the neighborhood likely to deteriorate in value (and pull down the value of the house)?

• Have you had the house checked by a construction expert (even if it is a new house)?

• How much money will you have to spend for repairs and improvements if you buy it?

• How much is the house worth to you—the top price you are willing to pay?

• If you must sell the house in a year or two, will you be able to get back what you paid for it, or close to it? (This is a good check on whether you are paying too much.)

• How long has the house been for sale? The longer it has been on the market, the more likely it can be bought at a reduced price.

• If you buy the house directly from the owner, will you get a break on the price (since the owner does not pay a real-estate broker's commission)?

• Finally, is the house priced right, or is it overpriced? Answer this question quickly and objectively, and it's probably the right answer. If you hem and haw, trying to think of reasons why the house may be worth the price asked, then it's probably overpriced.

The Unforeseen Expenses of Buying and Owning a House

• What are the total closing costs for the house? Can they be reduced? Have you compared them with closing costs at different banks?

• If you are buying a used house, can the existing title insurance be reissued to you at less than a new policy?

• How much must you pay in advance for escrow real-estate taxes?

• What are the total annual real-estate taxes for the house?

• If you are buying a new house, how much money will you need for inevitable moving-in expenses (grass seed, landscaping, new appliances, curtains, window shades, etc.)?

• If you are buying an old house, how much money will be needed for repairs and modernization?

- Have you arranged for a low-cost homeowners insurance policy?
- Do you have enough cash to buy the house and also pay for all moving-in expenses?
- Are the real-estate taxes likely to go up in the area? Putting it another way: Are new schools, new roads, sewers, and so on likely to be needed? Or are such services already there?

The Tight Mortgage Bind

- Have you talked to different mortgage-lenders to determine the best mortgage terms available? In other words, have you shopped around for the best mortgage deal?
- Have you considered a VA mortgage (if you are a veteran)? An FHA mortgage?
- Does the mortgage you are getting contain a prepayment privilege? An open-end clause? A provision for including appliance and household items in the mortgage?
- Will you be able to afford the monthly payment required to pay off the mortgage? Or should you get a longer-term mortgage with smaller monthly payments?
- Have you avoided possible mortgage traps, such as a small-print clause permitting the lender to raise the interest rate later? Also, a second mortgage trap, paying "points" for a VA or FHA mortgage?
- Will you avoid the tight mortgage bind?

The Vanishing Builder

- Have you checked on the credentials and past record of the builder?
- How long has the builder been established in business *locally*?
- Is the name of the builder's company, the firm you are legally buying the house from, the same name and same corporation he has used in the past?
- Have you talked with previous buyers of the builder's houses, asking them about their experiences with the builder?

- What kind of warranty do you get with the house?
- If it is a new house being financed with an FHA mortgage, will the house be covered by FHA's four-year protection against major defects?
- Does the builder really impress you as a well-established local builder who will be around in the future (as he was in the past)? Or does he stir suspicion in you that he is not as reliable as you would like?

The No-Design House

- Does the house have style and genuine good looks?
- Is the house a pure architectural style, all Colonial or any other traditional design? Or a true contemporary design?
- Does the house have good scale and proportion?
- Does the house have a good exposure, a good orientation in relation to the sun?
- Does the house take advantage of the best outdoor view?
- Is the house well located on its lot? Will you have privacy from the street and neighbors? Will the front area of the lot (the public zone) be easy to keep up and maintain? Will you have maximum use of your land on the sides of the house and in the back? Can you enter and leave the house quickly and conveniently?

The Garbled Floor Plan

- Does the floor plan provide good circulation in and out of the house and from one room to another?
- Are the main zones of the house—living, working, and sleeping—separated from each other?
- Do the number of floor levels—one and a half stories, two stories, or split level—offer the most advantages and greatest living convenience for your family?
- Is the interior of the house bright, cheerful, and attractive?
- Does the kitchen have a central location?
- Is the kitchen well designed? Does it have an efficient work triangle, plenty of counter space and storage, a good exposure, and enough space for eating?

- Is the bathroom (or bathrooms) ample and well designed and properly located for convenient access and privacy?
- Other rooms: Are they large enough? Are they designed for adequate furniture placement?
- Are the windows large enough? Are they properly located to give ample light and a feeling of spaciousness without loss of privacy?
- Are the closets large enough? Is there plenty of storage for household items, linen, and laundry as well as for clothing and personal possessions?

The Old-House Lemon

- Has the house been checked by a construction expert to determine if it is in structurally good condition?
- Does the price of the house compare favorably with the price of a comparable new house?
- How much money will it cost to repair, improve, and if necessary, modernize the house? Do you have fairly accurate estimates for such work?
- How much of a total dollar investment will the house require (sales price plus total estimated cost for improvements and repairs)? Will this total investment cause the house to be over-improved for its neighborhood?
- Do you *feel* that the house is in good condition and one that you really like and want?

The Marginal House

- Does the construction of the house conform with FHA's Minimum Property Requirements, at the very least?
- Does the house rate high in quality features for the following important parts?

    Foundation walls.

    Adequate termite safeguards.

    Rugged, low-upkeep exterior walls and paint.

    Tough interior wall surfaces.

    Well-made, closely fitted flooring that will retain its appearance.

    Top-quality national-brand windows and doors.

Kitchen countertop of a good plastic laminate (such as Formica), good kitchen cabinets, ample lighting and wiring outlets, and good ventilation.

Good-quality bathroom fixtures and accessories—that is, good lavatory, tub, toilet, faucets, shower nozzle, waterproof walls and floors.

Plumbing with ¾-to-1-inch supply from the street and copper or bronze piping.

Water heater large enough for your family with a ten-year warranty.

Septic tank of 900 to 1,000 gallons capacity and adequate leaching field, based on a percolation test that shows that the septic system will work in your ground.

Adequate electric wiring capacity: at least 240 volts and 100 amperes capacity, fifteen to twenty wiring circuits, plus spare circuits for future electric appliances.

A good roofing material of adequate weight and seal-down roof shingles.

Door hardware of solid brass, solid bronze, or solid aluminum, with a deadlock mechanism on exterior doors.

The Discomfort House

• Are the walls, ceilings, and if necessary, the floor, adequately insulated? Does the insulation conform with minimum R value standards?

• Is the house lined with a vapor barrier?

• In a new house is the heating system guaranteed to maintain the house at 70 degrees when the outdoor temperature is at its coldest locally? In other words, is the system large enough for the house?

• Is the heating equipment of good, if not top, quality?

• Is the heating distribution system properly designed and installed—for example, perimeter ducts and exterior floor outlets with warm-air heat, plenty of baseboard radiation with hot-water heat, and medium- or low-density baseboards with electric heat?

• Does the heating system produce heat quickly and operate quietly? (Turn it on and see.)

- Is the fuel used, whether it's gas or oil, economical in your area? If electric heat is used, what is its estimated annual operating cost for the house?
- If the house is centrally air-conditioned, is the system capacity large enough for the house? The cooling system should be guaranteed to maintain the indoor air at no more than 75 degrees and 50-percent relative humidity when the outdoor heat is at its summer peak for your climate.
- Is the insulation adequate for air conditioning?
- Are large window areas shaded from hot sunshine to keep down heat entry, hence keep down the cooling bills?
- If it is a new house without central air conditioning, are provisions made for inexpensive installation of cooling later? Ducts and furnace blower should be large enough for cooling, a cooling-coil plenum should be installed in advance, and a spare electric circuit of adequate capacity should be installed for future air conditioning.

The Gimmick House

- Does the house contain special eye-catching features that may seem to have special appeal but are not necessarily of special merit? In other words, are you attracted, unknowingly perhaps, by gimmick features?
- Do certain special features in the house tend to make you want to buy the house? Are they features that you can provide yourself in another, perhaps better, house at comparatively lower cost? Or are they intrinsic features that make it a really good house?
- What are the fundamental reasons why you and your family want a house and want the particular house you are considering?
- Have you thoroughly considered the kind of house you really want and need?
- Besides being of good design and construction, is the house one that you will really like and be satisfied with?

Index

Page numbers in italics refer to illustrations.